N. T. WRIGHT
FOR EVERYONE
BIBLE STUDY GUIDES

REVELATION

22 STUDIES FOR INDIVIDUALS AND GROUPS

N. T. WRIGHT

WITH KRISTIE BERGLUND

IVP Connect

An imprint of InterVarsity Press
Downers Grove, Illinois

InterVarsity Press
P.O. Box 1400, Downers Grove, IL 60515-1426
World Wide Web: www.ivpress.com
E-mail: email@ivpress.com

This study guide is based on and includes excerpts adapted from Revelation for Everyone, © 2011 Nicholas Thomas Wright. All New Testament quotations, unless otherwise indicated, are taken from The Kingdom New Testament published in the United States by HarperOne and from The New Testament for Everyone published in England by SPCK; copyright © 2011 by Nicholas Thomas Wright. Used by permission of SPCK, London. All rights reserved.

InterVarsity Press® is the book-publishing division of InterVarsity Christian Fellowship/USA®, a movement of students and faculty active on campus at hundreds of universities, colleges and schools of nursing in the United States of America, and a member movement of the International Fellowship of Evangelical Students. For information about local and regional activities, write Public Relations Dept., InterVarsity Christian Fellowship/USA, 6400 Schroeder Rd., P.O. Box 7895, Madison, WI 53707-7895, or visit the IVCF website at <www.intervarsity.org>.

Cover design: Cindy Kiple
Cover image: Pierre-Yves Babelon/Getty Images

ISBN 978-0-8308-2199-0

Printed in the United States of America ∞

P   20   19   18   17   16   15   14   13   12   11   10   9   8   7   6

Y   29   28   27   26   25   24   23   22   21   20   19   18   17

CONTENTS

GETTING THE MOST
OUT OF REVELATION

Many people today regard Revelation as the hardest book in the New Testament. It is full of strange, lurid, and sometimes bizarre and violent imagery. You might have thought that in a world of clever movies and DVDs, stuffed full of complex imaginative imagery, we would take to Revelation like ducks to water, but it doesn't always seem to work that way. As a result, many people who are quite at home in the Gospels, Acts and Paul find themselves tiptoeing around Revelation with a sense that they don't really belong there. But they do!

This book in fact offers one of the clearest and sharpest visions of God's ultimate purpose for the whole creation, and of the way in which the powerful forces of evil, at work in a thousand ways but not least in idolatrous and tyrannous political systems, can be and are being overthrown through the victory of Jesus the Messiah and the consequent costly victory of his followers. The world we live in today is no less complex and dangerous than the world of the late first century when this book was written, and we owe it to ourselves to get our heads and our hearts around Revelation's glorious pictures as we attempt to be faithful witnesses to God's love in a world of violence, hatred and suspicion.

John, its author—sometimes called "John the Seer" or "John the Divine," sometimes (probably wrongly) identified with the John who wrote the Gospel and epistles—is picking up a way of writing well known in the Jewish world of the time. This way of writing was designed to correspond to, and make available, the visions and "revelations" seen by holy, prayer-ful people who were wrestling with the question of the divine purpose.

Like a theater audience, God's people felt themselves in the dark. As they studied their ancient Scriptures and said their prayers, they be-lieved that the music was building up to something, but nobody was quite sure what. But then, like someone all by themselves in a theater for the first performance, the *seer*—the word reflects the reality, "one who sees" something that other people do not—finds that the curtain is suddenly pulled up. In a flash the seer is witnessing a scene, is in fact invited to be part of a scene, within God's ongoing drama.

Revelation—the idea, and this book—are based on the ancient Jew-ish belief that God's sphere of being and operation (heaven) and our sphere (earth) are not after all separated by a great gulf. They meet and merge and meld into one another in all kinds of ways. For ancient Jews, the place where this happened supremely was the temple in Jerusalem; this is not unimportant as the action proceeds. Most humans seem blind to this, only seeing the earthly side of the story. Some are aware that there is more to life, but are not quite sure what it's all about. Ancient Jews struggled to see both sides of the story, though it was often too much of an effort.

There are several things we learn in the very first verses of the book. First, this book is a four-stage *revelation*. It is about something God has revealed to Jesus himself and which Jesus is then passing on, via an an-gel, to "his servants" through one particular servant, John (Revelation 1:1). God—Jesus—angel—John—churches. These lines get blurred as the book goes on, but the framework remains basic.

Second, the book takes the form of an extended *letter*. There are par-ticular letters in chapters 2 and 3 to the seven churches in western Tur-key, but the book as a whole is a letter from John to all the churches, telling them what he has seen (Revelation 1:4).

Third, the book is a *prophecy* (Revelation 1:3). Like many prophets in ancient Israel, John draws freely on earlier biblical traditions. These were in themselves revelations of God and his purposes. Again and again, they come up fresh, in new forms.

Fourth, the book functions as *witness* (Revelation 1:2). Here we meet a familiar problem. The Greek words for "witness" and "testimony" are basically the same, but it's hard to settle on one of these English words to the exclusion of the other. We should, though, remember two things whenever we see either word.

They regularly carry a sense that God is ultimately conducting a great heavenly lawcourt. In that lawcourt, the "witness" borne by Jesus and his followers is a key to the ultimate judgment and verdict.

They regularly carry the sense which the Greek original word, *martyr*, has given to the English language. Those who bear this "testimony" may well be called to suffer, or even to die, for what they have said.

Fifth, and far and away the most important: everything that is to come flows from the central figure, Jesus himself, and ultimately from God the Father, "He Who Is and Who Was and Who Is to Come" (Revelation 1:4, 8). Even in this short opening John manages to unveil a good deal of what he believes about God and Jesus, and about the divine plan. God is the Almighty, the beginning and the end (Revelation 1:8); Alpha and Omega are the first and last letters of the Greek alphabet, and this title occurs at the beginning and the end of John's book (see 22:13). Other lords and rulers will claim similar titles, but there is only one God to whom they belong.

(For more on this book of the Bible, also see my *Revelation for Everyone* published by SPCK and Westminster John Knox, on which this guide is based. New Testament quotations in this guide are from my own translation, published as *The Kingdom New Testament* by HarperOne in the United States and published as *The New Testament for Everyone* by SPCK in England.)

When John was writing Revelation, the early Christian movement grew and developed momentum throughout the latter part of the first century. Still, many questions emerged. What was God doing now? What were his plans for the little churches dotted around the Mediterranean world? Where was it all going?

In particular, why was God allowing followers of Jesus to suffer persecution? What line should they take when faced with the fastest growing "religion" of the time, namely, the worship of Caesar, the Roman emperor? Should they resist?

There may have been several groups of Christians in ancient Turkey, where John seems to have been based. They would have been mostly poor, meeting in one another's homes. By contrast, people were building grand and expensive temples for Caesar and his family in various cities, eager to show Rome how loyal they were. What would Jesus himself say about this? Did it mean that, after all, the Christians were wasting their time, following a crucified Jew rather than the one who was rather obviously the "lord of the world"?

As we will see through this guide (prepared with the help of Kristie Berglund, for which I am grateful), Revelation is written to say *no* to that last question—and to say much more besides. At its center is a fresh "revelation of Jesus the Messiah" (1:1). John, with his head and his heart full of Israel's Scriptures, discovered on one particular occasion, as he was praying, that the curtain was pulled back. He found himself face to face with Jesus himself.

SUGGESTIONS FOR INDIVIDUAL STUDY

1. As you begin each study, pray that God will speak to you through his Word.

2. Read the introduction to the study and respond to the "Open" question that follows it. This is designed to help you get into the theme of the study.

3. Read and reread the Bible passage to be studied. Each study is designed to help you consider the meaning of the passage in its context. The commentary and questions in this guide are based on my own translation of each passage found in the companion volume to this guide in the For Everyone series on the New Testament (published by SPCK and Westminster John Knox).

4. Write your answers to the questions in the spaces provided or in a personal journal. Each study includes three types of questions: obser-

vation questions, which ask about the basic facts in the passage; interpretation questions, which delve into the meaning of the passage; and application questions, which help you discover the implications of the text for growing in Christ. Writing out your responses can bring clarity and deeper understanding of yourself and of God's Word.

5. Each session features selected comments from the For Everyone series. These notes provide further biblical and cultural background and contextual information. They are designed not to answer the questions for you but to help you along as you study the Bible for yourself. For even more reflections on each passage, you may wish to have on hand a copy of the companion volume from the For Everyone series as you work through this study guide.

6. Use the guidelines in the "Pray" section to focus on God, thanking him for what you have learned and praying about the applications that have come to mind.

SUGGESTIONS FOR GROUP MEMBERS

1. Come to the study prepared. Follow the suggestions for individual study mentioned above. You will find that careful preparation will greatly enrich your time spent in group discussion.

2. Be willing to participate in the discussion. The leader of your group will not be lecturing. Instead, she or he will be asking the questions found in this guide and encouraging the members of the group to discuss what they have learned.

3. Stick to the topic being discussed. These studies focus on a particular passage of Scripture. Only rarely should you refer to other portions of the Bible or outside sources. This allows for everyone to participate on equal ground and for in-depth study.

4. Be sensitive to the other members of the group. Listen attentively when they describe what they have learned. You may be surprised by their insights! Each question assumes a variety of answers. Many questions do not have "right" answers, particularly questions that

aim at meaning or application. Instead the questions push us to explore the passage more thoroughly.

When possible, link what you say to the comments of others. Also, be affirming whenever you can. This will encourage some of the more hesitant members of the group to participate.

5. Be careful not to dominate the discussion. We are sometimes so eager to express our thoughts that we leave too little opportunity for others to respond. By all means participate! But allow others to also.

6. Expect God to teach you through the passage being discussed and through the other members of the group. Pray that you will have an enjoyable and profitable time together, but also that as a result of the study you will find ways that you can take action individually and/ or as a group.

7. It will be helpful for groups to follow a few basic guidelines. These guidelines, which you may wish to adapt to your situation, should be read at the beginning of the first session.

   • Anything said in the group is considered confidential and will not be discussed outside the group unless specific permission is given to do so.

   • We will provide time for each person present to talk if he or she feels comfortable doing so.

   • We will talk about ourselves and our own situations, avoiding conversation about other people.

   • We will listen attentively to each other.

   • We will be very cautious about giving advice.

Additional suggestions for the group leader can be found at the back of the guide.

PROPONTIS

Sardis The seven churches
Antioch Other cities
- - - - - - Roads

Troas

Lesbos

Pergamum

Thyatira

A S I A

(Pisidian)
Antioch

Chios

Sardis

Philadelphia

Smyrna

Aegean Sea

Ephesus

Hierapolis

Laodicea

Colossae

Miletus

Patmos

0   50 miles

0   50   100 kms

Rhodes

The Seven Churches of Asia

1

JESUS REVEALED

Revelation 1

Some years ago there was an eclipse of the sun. These things happen rarely enough, and to witness it is a great experience. But staring at the sun, as it slips behind the moon and then emerges the other side, is dangerous. If you look through binoculars, or a telescope, the sun's power on your eye can do permanent damage. It can even cause blindness.

On this particular occasion, there were public warnings broadcast on radio and television, and printed in the newspapers, to the effect that people should be careful. Only look, they said, through special dark glasses. Eventually one person, who obviously had very little understanding of natural phenomena, got cross about all this. Surely, they thought, this was a "health and safety" issue. A letter was sent to the London *Times:* if this event was so dangerous, why was the government allowing it in the first place?

Fortunately, even the most totalitarian of governments has not yet been able to control what the sun and the moon get up to. But the danger of full-power sunlight is worth contemplating as we hear John speaking about his vision of Jesus.

OPEN

Have you ever stared at the sun for just a moment too long? What effect did it have on you?

STUDY

1. *Read Revelation 1:1-8.* Who is this book all about and what do we learn about him in these opening verses?

2. What does it mean that this book serves as a "testimony" or "witness" (v. 2)?

3. Even in this short opening John manages to unveil a good deal of what he believes about God and Jesus, and about the divine plan. God is the Almighty, the beginning and the end. Other "lords" and rulers will claim similar titles, but there is only one God to whom they belong.

    What other "lords" in our own day make competing claims to the Almighty status that—as John testifies here—in reality belongs to God alone?

4. *Read Revelation 1:9-20.* Where is John when he writes this letter and why is he there?

5. Why would this be important to John's original readers?

6. Exile has given John time to pray, to reflect, and now to receive the most explosive vision of God's power and love. How have you experienced God's power and love in the midst of painful or distressing situations?

7. What does John see when he turns to find out who is speaking to him (vv. 12-16)?

8. This vision of Jesus draws together the vision of two characters in one of the most famous biblical visions, that of Daniel 7. There, as the suffering of God's people reaches its height, "the Ancient of Days" takes his seat in heaven, and "one like a son of man" (in other words, a human figure, representing God's people and, in a measure, all the human race) is presented before him, and enthroned alongside him. Now, in John's vision, these two pictures seem to have merged. When we are looking at Jesus, he is saying, we are looking straight through him at the Father himself.

   Why is it significant for us that the one who represents humanity and the God who rules above all come together in the person of Jesus?

9. What is John's response when he sees this vision of the "one like a son of man" in the midst of the lampstands (v. 17)?

10. Why does Jesus emphasize that he is the "living one" who holds "the keys of death and Hades" (vv. 17-18)?

11. Seven is the number of perfection, and the seven churches listed in verse 11 stand for all churches in the world, all places and all times. The seven churches need to know that Jesus himself is standing in their midst, and that the "angels" who represent and look after each of them are held in his right hand.

How might this vision of Jesus in the midst of the churches have comforted suffering believers in the first century?

12. How does it bring comfort to us today?

PRAY

Hold the picture of Jesus in your mind, detail by detail. Let those eyes of flame search you in and out. Imagine standing beside a huge waterfall, its noise like sustained thunder, and imagine that noise as a human voice, echoing around the hills and round your head. And then imagine his hand reaching out to touch you and his voice speaking the words, "Do not be afraid." Take comfort in his presence. Give him thanks for revealing himself to you and ask that you might have eyes to see him as he truly is.

NOTE ON REVELATION 1:1

The word *revelation* has come to be used as the title for the book (not "revelations" in the plural, please note). This is partly because the original word, *apocalypse*, wasn't well known at the time of earlier translations into English. Now, of course, *apocalypse*, and its cousin *apocalyptic*, have become well known in English. Perhaps too well known: they have come to refer not so much to the sudden unveiling of previously hidden truth, but to major events, violent and disturbing events such as natural disasters (earthquakes, volcanoes, tsunamis) or major and horrific human actions such as genocide in Cambodia or Rwanda.

But that isn't quite the sense that *revelation* or *apocalypse* has in this book. John is picking up a way of writing well known in the Jewish world of the time. As mentioned earlier, this way of writing was designed to correspond to, and make available, the visions and "revelations" seen by holy, prayerful people who were wrestling with the question of the divine purpose.

2

LETTERS TO EPHESUS, SMYRNA, PERGAMUM AND THYATIRA

Revelation 2

I was involved some years ago in making a series of radio programs where people from quite different backgrounds came together for an hour to discuss complex and challenging topics of the day. Since this was being made by the British Broadcasting Corporation (BBC), there were some in-house guidelines. We were not supposed, for instance, to recommend particular brand-name products on air, since the publicly funded BBC does not advertise.

But I had not expected to be pulled up short simply for answering one of the questions. A listener had written in, asking the panel, "If you could choose your religious faith, what would it be, and why?" Since I was the only obvious "religious" representative on the panel, the person chairing the discussion asked me to speak first. In my opening fifty seconds, I tried to make three points. First, I said that Christianity isn't exactly a "religion" in the sense people mean today; it's much bigger than that, much more all-embracing. Then I pointed out that hardly anyone actually "chooses" a faith, like someone in a supermarket picking out a particular brand of soup. Then I began to say why, granted all that, I would argue for the truth of the Christian faith and for the positive, healing, life-giving effect it has. I was only a few words into that third section, which was after all answering the question, when I was interrupted by the chair. "Oh, Tom," she said, "we can't say that sort of thing on air. That's proselytizing."

Western society has become like that BBC employee: paranoid about any actual claims, not only that we might have the truth but that someone else might not. And then we read the New Testament and we find passages like this one in Revelation 2: "I know the blasphemy of those self-styled Jews." We recoil. How can anyone say such things?

OPEN

Do you sometimes hesitate to speak up about things you really believe in out of fear that you might offend someone? Explain.

STUDY

1. *Read Revelation 2:1-7.* What words of praise, warning and promise are spoken to the church at Ephesus?

    Praise, warning, promise

    Nicolaitans - heretics, idol worship.

2. The Ephesian believers have drawn a clear line between those who are really following Jesus and those who are not (v. 2). As all church workers know, a group that is rightly concerned for the truth of the gospel may forget that the very heart of that gospel is love. What can we do to help maintain this delicate balance between truth and love in our own churches today?

    — Vigilent, doctrinally strong,

    — lost zeal for the faith,

3. *Read Revelation 2:8-11.* In the church at Smyrna, the Lord finds nothing to condemn. What seems to be the main focus of this letter?

4. The Jewish synagogue in Smyrna has become a "satan-synagogue"— not just in a vague, general, abusive sense, but in the rather sharply defined sense that, as "the satan" is literally "the accuser," the synagogue in town has been "accusing" the Christians of all kinds of wickedness. What is the Lord's advice to the church at Smyrna when it comes to responding to such accusations and their consequences (v. 10)?

5. How might we take the promise of verse 11 to heart and live as those who know that the "second death" has no power to harm the faithful?

6. *Read Revelation 2:12-17.* How does the Lord refer to the city of Pergamum in this letter (v. 13)? *Satan has his throne. True - standing up in the face of persecution.*

7. Why might it have been particularly difficult to be a Christian in this kind of place? *Persecution ⟹ temptation —*

This church basically made the same mistake that the Israelites committed when King Balak of Moab hired the prophet Balaam to curse Israel (v. 14; see Numbers 22–24). Balaam found he couldn't curse them; he was, to that extent, a true prophet. But he still wanted Balak's promised reward, and so he encouraged the king to use a different tactic. Where direct spiritual attack (the curse) had failed, more subtle temptation might work; and, as often, the best temptation would be sexual. In an ancient version of the "honey-trap" beloved

Sexual — Monogamous

of spy novels (and, for all I know, actual spying), Moabite women were sent to entice the Israelite men—who, presumably, already had Israelite wives. Through this means, the Israelites were drawn into idolatry, worshiping gods other than Yahweh.

→ Idolatry → Adaltery — Sex —

8. The problem in Pergamum is that much of the church has lost its cutting edge, its ability to say no to the surrounding culture. For these people, Jesus has stern words. How do we take this warning seriously and not succumb to societal pressures that lead us away from following Jesus purely and faithfully?

Grace is there | → But say no to the surrounding Culture.

9. *Read Revelation 2:18-29.* John praises the church at Thyatira and criticizes it (vv. 19-20). Why would the church need both?

Deeds matter

10. In the previous letter the problem in the church at Pergamum was identified by allusion to a famous biblical figure, Balaam the prophet. This time another ancient villain plays the same role: Jezebel, the wife of King Ahab, who seems to have been the cause of at least some of her husband's wickedness. Their story is told in 1 Kings 16–22, ending with Ahab's death; Jezebel's own story comes to its unpleasant end in 2 Kings 9. Jezebel, like the women of Moab whom Balaam and Balak used to seduce the Israelite men away from the pure worship of Yahweh, was a foreign woman who introduced the worship of Baal, a rival god, into Israel. That was at the heart of many other evils, summarized in 2 Kings 9:22 as "whoredoms and sorceries."

What might have caused believers at Thyatira to fall prey to this kind of deception?

Thank you! Conviction; warning

11. What is required at the moment, for those who have not been drawn away by the teaching and practices of "Jezebel," is that they "hold on tightly." That is a word for all those Christians today who find themselves in churches and fellowships where teaching and behavior which they know is not the way of the Messiah is being eagerly embraced and hailed as God-given.

Chris Wolfe's Ministry — marriage —

What challenges like this is the church generally or your fellowship in particular facing today?

12. How might we "hold on tightly" in the face of these?

PRAY

Give thanks to the Lord for the ways he both encourages and rebukes us—and all his churches everywhere—so that we might live well as his people in the world. Ask that he might give you strength to hold tightly to him even in the face of great temptation to wander away from his truth and love. Pray that you might be among those who "conquer" and experience the fulfillment of God's promises.

NOTE ON REVELATION 2:6 AND 15

The church in Ephesus is commended for refusing to tolerate "the Nicolaitans" (v. 6). These people crop up again in the letter to Pergamum (v. 15), where again nothing more is said to identify who they were or what they were teaching (that's the point in the Pergamum letter) and doing (that's the point in the Ephesian one). Various attempts have been made, in the ancient church and in modern scholarship, to figure this out, with hardly any success. It may be that "the Nicolaitans" are, in fact, a small group who are teaching something very like this "teaching of Balaam" (v. 14). Some have suggested that, in the original languages, the names *Balaam* and *Nicolas* may have similar meanings. The main point we can gain from this mention of the "Nicolaitans" is that the church must always be on the lookout for individuals or groups who try to teach strange new ideas or to introduce strange new practices. This doesn't mean that God never has new things for the church to learn; far from it. But these new things will come from prayerful, Spirit-filled study of Scripture, not through mere innovation.

NOTE ON REVELATION 2:13

Why is Pergamum described as where the satan has its throne? Pergamum was a center of Roman imperial rule and cult, and John sees behind the pomp and the purple to the dark spiritual reality of satanic rule which has enabled the empire to impose itself across so much of the world.

NOTE ON REVELATION 2:17

What is the secret manna and the white stone? On the wilderness journey after escaping Egypt (when Balaam sought to curse Israel), God fed his people with manna, bread that dropped down from the sky. I will do the same for you, promises Jesus here. Many Christians have clung on to this promise as they find themselves spiritually hungry in an alien environment. Many, too, have seen it as a pointer to the sacrament of Jesus' body and blood, which again parallels 1 Corinthians 10.

Regarding the white stone with a new name written on it, Pergamum's great buildings were made of a dark, black local stone. When people wanted to put up inscriptions, they obtained white marble on which to carve them. This was then fixed to the black buildings, where it stood out all the more clearly. In addition there was a custom of guests at a feast being given a stone with their name on as a ticket of admission.

3

LETTERS TO SARDIS, PHILADELPHIA AND LAODICEA

Revelation 3

You might be surprised to know that, in some parts of England, "The Wars of the Roses" still live on. These wars were fought between the Houses of York (the white rose) and Lancaster (the red rose) in the fifteenth century. Even today, whenever Yorkshire meets Lancashire on the cricket field, the game is known as "the Roses Match" and old loyalties are stirred once again.

From the fifteenth century to the twenty-first is a long time. But if we in our modern world have long memories, they are as nothing beside the memory of great events cherished, for good or ill, by many in the ancient world. People might not have been able to tell you exactly when an event took place—it might have been, at the most, "in the reign of King such-and-such"—but they knew more or less what had happened, allowing for some pardonable embellishment here and there.

OPEN

What are some events in the distant history of your family, your church or your nation that continue to shape your life today?

STUDY

1. *Read Revelation 3:1-6.* What are the charges against the church at Sardis (vv. 1-2)?

2. What does it mean that this church's works were "incomplete" in God's sight?

3. The residents of Sardis knew very well what had happened to their city six hundred years before the Christian gospel reached them. The city had been thought, for a long time, completely impregnable. Until one night the invading Persian army found a way in. Someone, greatly daring, got up part of the sheer cliff and managed a surprise attack. Because nobody was expecting it, the result was all the more devastating. Cyrus the Persian, who features in various biblical stories as well, conquered Sardis in 546 B.C.: a never-to-be-forgotten moment. Though Sardis remained an important city, the lesson seemingly had been learned.

   What words of Jesus in this letter are intended to remind the church at Sardis of this lesson from their history?

   Learn. the lesson of your history. You are vulnerable.

4. How might we heed the call to wake up and strengthen what remains of our own works before it's too late?

   temptation of the world.   habits

5. *Read Revelation 3:7-13.* Why does Jesus praise the Philadelphian church (vv. 8, 10)?

6. As in the letter to Smyrna we have an indication that the synagogue community was using its civic status to block the advance of the message about Israel's Messiah, Jesus. Why did some Jews find the message of Jesus to be very Jewish and others find it to be challenging to the Jewish faith?

7. The first Christians, partly because of Jesus and partly because of the gift of the Spirit, regarded themselves as the true temple, the place where the living God had made his home. Sometimes the Jerusalem leaders had themselves been called pillars. But now it is the ordinary Christians in Philadelphia who are to be pillars (v. 12)—in a city notorious for danger from earthquakes!

Why might this have been a promise the Philadelphians would cherish?

Hope through difficulty, disappointment

8. Equipped with regal power, Jesus has opened a door right in front of the Philadelphia Christians (v. 8) and he is urging them to go through it. The meaning is almost certainly that they have an opportunity not just to stand firm but to make advances, to take the good news of Jesus into places and hearts where it has not yet reached.

What open doors is Jesus setting before us today?

Doors opening? Give more
An open door. Offering down during pandemic

9. *Read Revelation* 3:14-22. Often being even-handed and moderate
    in difficult situations is a virtue. Why is that not the case for the
    church at Laodicea (v. 16)?

    $20,000

10. When an earthquake in A.D. 61 did major damage to several cities in
    the Lycus valley, to the south of Philadelphia, one city was able to
    refuse imperial help. It was a proud thing to do. Most would have
    jumped at the offer. But Laodicea reckoned it didn't need outside
    help. It was quite rich enough, thank you very much. Apparently the
    smug, well-off attitude of the town as a whole had rubbed off on the
    Christians.

    How were the Laodicean Christians blinded by their riches?

    no conviction not generous not charitable *not wrong but not alive too comfortable*

11. In what ways are we overly influenced by the attitudes and opinions
    of those around us?

    Bad water, not good for drinking or for bathing.

12. What does it mean to you that Jesus would come and sit down and
    have a meal with those who hear his voice (v. 20)?

    Temptation is to spend your money on silly, self-indulgent things. Jesus is available. Accessible

PRAY

These letters provide opportunities for us both to confess the ways in which we have fallen short of our calling as Christians and to renew our trust in God's promises to us. Reflecting on the shortcomings of these churches—the incompleteness of their works, the blindness to their true condition—confess to God the ways your own shortcomings keep you from fully participating in the work of joyful witness to Christ. Give thanks to God for the wonderful promises he has made and commit yourself once again to trusting fully in him.

NOTE ON REVELATION 3:3

Will this "coming" be the final Day, the "second coming" properly understood? Probably not, though that too is in view as the ultimate backdrop. Throughout this book we glimpse other "comings," which may consist in times of persecution (when Jesus is "coming" to cleanse and purify his church) or of moments of comfort and restoration. Even Laodicea is promised that if they open the door he will "come in to them and eat with them" (v. 20). Here in 3:3 it seems that the coming may well be a time of persecution or simply of internal collapse, a church quietly drowning in its own inoffensiveness, unable to believe that its reputation for being alive is no longer deserved.

NOTE ON REVELATION 3:9

This verse is considerably harsher than the equivalent in the Smyrna letter (2:9). We remind ourselves again that it is not anti-Jewish; what we have here is what we might call an inner-Jewish question. Which of these groups can properly claim to be the true Jews, bearing the torch of God's ancient people? This, as we saw, was a common enough question in other parts of first-century Judaism. Here Jesus is quite clear. Those who follow him, the Davidic Messiah, are the true Jews. Those who deny him are forfeiting their right to that noble name.

Responsibility to open the door.
Receive Him here.

PRAISE TO THE CREATOR

Revelation 4

Scientists and anthropologists have often asked themselves, "What is it that humans can do that computers can't do?" The writer David Lodge wrote a powerful novel on this theme, entitled *Thinks . . .* The heroine eventually discovers the answer: humans can weep; and humans can forgive. Those are two very powerful and central human activities. They take place in quite a different dimension from anything a computer can do.

A similar question is often posed: "What can humans do that animals can't do?" Again, some scientists have tried to insist that we humans are simply "naked apes," a more sophisticated version, perhaps, but still within the same continuum. This is a trickier question than the one about computers, but to get straight to the point: the main difference, as twenty-four elders in Revelation 4 demonstrate, is that humans can say the word *because*. In particular, they can say it about God himself.

OPEN

In your experience with your own pets or with other animals, how do they compare with human beings? What are the main similarities and differences?

Soul, Reason, Conscious ness, self conscious ness

STUDY

1. *Read Revelation 4:1-5.* What is meant by the invitation John is given
   (v. 1)?

   Reveal what must take place.

   Show you -

2. "Heaven" and "earth" are not separated by a great gulf in the Bible
   as they are in much popular imagination. Heaven, God's sphere of
   reality, is right here, close beside us, intersecting with our ordinary
   reality. How might this understanding shape the way we think about
   the "door in heaven" that John sees?

   Different dimension.

   Nearness -

3. What difference does it make in our everyday life of faith to embrace
   the fact that God's sphere of reality is not so far away at all?

   Close -
   accessible - *Still ground but*
   cares to reveal things

4. The invitation to "come up" and see what's going on does not, as
   some people have supposed, have anything to do with God's people
   being snatched away to heaven to avoid awful events that are about
   to take place on earth. It is about a prophet being taken into God's
   throne room so that he can see behind the scenes and understand
   both what is going to take place and how it all fits together and
   makes sense. Like some of the ancient Israelite prophets, John is
   privileged to stand in God's council chamber and hear what is going
   on in order to report it to his people back on earth. Like Micaiah bin
   Imlah in 1 Kings 22, he sees God himself sitting on his throne, with
   his hosts around him, and is privy to their discussions and plans.
   But this scene reminds us too of Ezekiel 1, where the prophet is
   given a vision of God's throne-chariot, carried to and fro on whirl-

ing, fiery wheels. The rainbow (v. 3 of our present passage) reminds us of that, but also takes us back to the story of Noah.

Take a moment to read and reflect on Genesis 9:8-13. Why is it significant that John describes the rainbow (v. 3) as being visible in the throne room—encircling the very place where God is seated and rules over the earth?

rainbow is a promise.
reminder of God's promise.

rainbow is decomposition of light

5. Who sits on the thrones gathered around God's throne and why are there twenty-four of them?

Larger reality, behind what we customarily see.

6. Behind the ambiguous struggles and difficulties of ordinary Christians—there stands the heavenly throne room in which the world's Creator and Lord remains sovereign. Spend a few moments contemplating John's vision of this reality. How does it help you to understand better our own present circumstances?

God is on his throne, no matter what is happening here on earth.

7. *Read Revelation 4:6-11.* How does John describe the four creatures surrounding the throne (vv. 6-8)?

eyes - watchfulness - everything is seen.
lion, ox, man, eagle

The four creatures deserve our attention. They represent the animal creation, including humans but at this stage with the human-faced creature being simply one among the others, alongside the king of the wild beasts (the lion), the massive leader of tamed animals (the ox) and the undisputed king of the birds (the eagle). These remark- able creatures seem to be not merely surrounding God's throne but ready to do his bidding. *Animals subject to God's bidding*

Life processes

8. Twice John tells us that these creatures are "full of eyes" (vv. 6, 8). What is implied by this image?

   all seeing.
   All knowing.
   Nothing goes unseen

9. Which of God's attributes do the creatures emphasize in their song of praise (v. 8)?

   Holy, Almighty,
   past, present, future

The song of these creatures is simply an act of adoring praise. We are meant, reading this passage, to see with the psalmist that all creation is dependent on God and worships him in its own way. That alone is worth pondering as a striking contrast to how most of us view the animal kingdom. But the contrast with the twenty-four elders is then made all the more striking. Creation as a whole simply worships God; the humans who represent God's people understand *why they do so.*

10. According to the song of the elders (v. 11), why is God worthy of worship?

    God is in charge.

11. What can we learn from this passage about praising God as the Cre- ator of all things in our private prayers and public worship?

12. Humans are given the capacity to reflect, to understand what's going on. And, in particular, to express that understanding in worship. How might we be more intentional about allowing our thinking about God to inform our praise?

PRAY

All creation worships God; we humans are called to worship him with mind as well as heart, recognizing that he is worthy of all praise as the Creator of all things. Take time to offer thanksgiving and praise to God for the specific reasons why he is worthy of our worship, paying particular attention to the wonders of his creative work.

NOTE ON REVELATION 4:6

The final detail of this opening description of the throne room is "something like a sea of glass." This is deeply mysterious. Solomon's temple had a "sea," a huge bronze bowl (1 Kings 7:23-26), and this may have been part of the point. But in Revelation 15:2 the "sea of glass" has become more like the Red Sea, through which the children of Israel have passed to safety. The other sea in Revelation is the one from which, as in Daniel 7, the great beast emerges (13:1), while the dragon stands beside the shore apparently presiding over the beast's appearing (12:18). Then, of course, in the New Jerusalem itself there is "no longer any sea" (21:1). All this seems to indicate that the "sea" within the throne room is a kind of symbolic representation of the fact that, within God's world as it currently is, evil is present and dangerous. But it is contained within God's sovereign purposes, and it will eventually be overthrown.

5

WORTHY IS THE LAMB! *[handwritten arrow]*

Revelation 5 *[handwritten: 2 weeks / Isolated]*

We stood and stared at the letter as it lay on the doormat. It was a smart envelope, good quality paper, with clear, bold typewritten name and address. And at the top, in even larger letters, we saw the words: *To Be Opened by Addressee Only*. And the addressee was not at home. We hardly dared touch it.

But supposing the envelope had said, *To Be Opened by the Person Who Deserves to Do So*? That would have been even more intriguing, and would have posed a different kind of challenge. How do you know if you deserve to open it? As one writer put it, we are all overdrawn at the moral bank. That is the situation at the start of this scene. We are still looking, through John's eyes, at the heavenly throne room, and it is not simply one long round of endless, repetitive praise. This is the throne room of God the Creator, and his world is not merely a tableau, a living picture to be enjoyed. It is a project. It is going somewhere. There is work to be done.

[handwritten: Scroll contains God's account of the course of history.]

OPEN

Have you ever been asked to do something or given something that you didn't feel you deserved? How did you respond?

[handwritten: Very blessed, I'm not really better than this person, to have lived the life I have lived,]

STUDY

1. *Read Revelation 5:1-7.* What does John see in the right hand of the one sitting on the throne and how does he describe it (v. 1)?

2. We rightly guess that the scroll contains God's secret plan to undo and overthrow the world-destroying projects that have already gained so much ground, and to plant and nurture instead the world-rescuing project which will get creation itself back on track in the right direction. What would it take for someone to be "worthy" to read such a proclamation?

    — *World rescuing project*

3. Why does John burst into tears and weep bitterly (v. 4)? _

    Uncertainty is tough. Disappointed to him out on God's plan.

4. How does John's reaction resonate with us as we look around at our world? *Uncertainty, future seem cloudy.*

    Hope. Scroll provides hope.
    Destiny of the world.

5. In verses 5-6 we come to one of the most decisive moments in all Scripture. What John has *heard* is the announcement of the Lion. What he then *sees* is the Lamb. What are the differences between these two animals?

    Jesus   — Lion

6. What does each one symbolize?

[handwritten: Lion victory accomplished by sacrifice of the lamb.]

From this moment on, John, and we as his careful readers, are to understand that the victory won by the Lion is accomplished through the sacrifice of the Lamb, and in no other way. But we are also to understand that what has been accomplished by the Lamb's sacrifice is not merely the wiping away of sin for a few people here and there. The victory won by the Lamb is God's Lion-like victory over all the forces of corruption and death, over everything that would destroy and obliterate God's good, powerful and lovely creation.

[handwritten: 4 generations lineage ~420 years]

7. *Read Revelation 5:8-14. What happens when the Lamb takes the scroll?*

[handwritten: elders fall down. horns + power eyes - complete vision.]

8. Why are the elders holding harps and bowls of incense in the presence of the Lamb (v. 8)?

[handwritten: prayers of the saints]

9. How does this scene invite us to participate in what is happening in the very throne room of God and the Lamb?

[handwritten: Overwhelming large group, very impressive.]

Any first-century Jew would know that "by his blood" meant "through his death seen as a sacrifice." Similarly they would know that a sacrifice through which God "purchased a people . . . and made them a kingdom and priests" is the ultimate Passover sacrifice, the final fulfillment of what God had done close up in history when he set his people free from their slavery in Egypt, "purchasing" them like slaves from a slave-market, in order to establish them as a "royal priesthood," as the people through whom he would accomplish his worldwide purposes (Exodus 19:4-6).

But John, as so often, isn't just echoing one biblical passage. This first song also echoes the great passage in Daniel 7 where, after the raging of the monsters and the vindication of the "one like a son of man," God establishes his rule over the whole earth in and through the "people of the holy ones of the Most High" (Daniel 7:22, 27). The rescue effected in Daniel is, as it were, the great new exodus, with the monsters who have oppressed God's people taking the part of Pharaoh in Egypt. John is picking up the same storyline, only now putting together the slaughtered Passover Lamb and the vindicated Son of Man.

10. How many creatures does John hear join in the third song of worship (v. 13)?

11. Why is it significant that in these songs the Lamb shares the worship which belongs, and uniquely and only belongs, to the one creator God?

12. In what ways might the expressions of worship found in these songs inform and inspire us as we too join in the worship of the Lamb?

PRAY

Join in singing the new song of all the elders, angels and creatures:

The slaughtered lamb has now deserved
To take the riches and the power,
To take the wisdom, strength, and honor,
To take the glory and the blessing.

As you bring your requests before God, trust that they are being offered before him as incense in his very throne room.

NOTE ON REVELATION 5:2-3

Nobody deserves to open the scroll. But that constitutes a major problem. God the Creator committed himself, back in Genesis 1 and 2, to work within his creation *through obedient humankind.* That is how the world was designed to work. If God then said, "Well, humans have failed, so I'll have to do it some other way," that would be to unmake the very structure of his good creation, to turn it into a different sort of world entirely. Someone must be found.

From within the traditions of Israel, one answer would have been: Israel itself is called to be God's true humanity, to put God's rescue plan into operation. True. But, though John doesn't say so explicitly, here we meet the second level of the problem. Israel too has failed, has let God down. And here again God appears to be faced with a dilemma. If he says, "Well, Israel hasn't done what I hoped, so I'll have to cut out that bit of my plan," it would look as though he has blundered, has been flailing around with different ideas, none of which have worked. God has, in other words, determined to *run* the world through *humans,* and to *rescue* the world through *Israel.* Both have let him down. What will God now do? We ought to be able to guess what the answer will be. God will provide a truly human one. God will provide a true Israelite. God will send the Messiah and he will fulfill in himself what humanity and Israel as a whole were called to accomplish.

6

THE DAY IS COMING

Revelation 6

All doctors, and all pastors, know that when someone comes to them with a problem, the problem they talk about may not be the only problem they have. The pain that gets someone into the doctor's office may well be only a symptom of much deeper ills, medical or psychological. The fear, depression or guilt that makes someone knock on the pastor's door is quite likely to be a second- or third-order anxiety which won't be solved until the first-order ones have been exposed and addressed.

This often lands the patient, or the person seeking counseling, in a position very like the reader of Revelation 6. We finally pluck up courage to go to the doctor. Now I'm going to feel well again, happy again! This visit will put me back on track! Wise doctors or pastors know that they must disappoint, for the moment, in order to get to the root of the problem and effect the lasting cure. First we must find out when you have felt like this before. What have you been most afraid of? Soon the person answering the questions will feel uncomfortable. I didn't know we were going to get into all *that*. Surely we don't need to bring those things up again? It was a long time ago, and besides . . .

Sorry, but we do need to. Unless we lay out the problems to their full extent, no real healing can take place. Unless the ills of the world are

Lay out the problems

[handwritten: Have hope —]

[handwritten: But It gets worse before it gets better.]

brought out, shown up in their true colors, put on display and allowed to do their worst, they cannot be overthrown. Unless the four horsemen ride out and do what they have to do, the scroll cannot be read. The victory of the Lion-Lamb will not be complete.

OPEN

Have you, or someone you know, ever gone for help for a particular symptom or problem only to discover that there was a more serious issue underlying it? Explain.

[handwritten: Serious issue underlying gets worse before it gets better.]

STUDY

1. *Read Revelation 6:1-8.* What does John see the Lamb begin to do (v. 1)?

   [handwritten: Open the first seal]

2. When the Lamb opens the first four seals of the scroll, instead of four glorious remedies for the world's ills, we find the four living creatures summoning four horses and riders, each (so it seems) to make matters worse. How are these horsemen described and what does each seem to represent?

   [handwritten: white 1. bow, crown, conquest]
   [handwritten: red 2 sword, war, exchange, economy]
   [handwritten: black 3. scale, Death, Hades, famine, plague, wild beasts]
   [handwritten: pale]

3. What is the fourth horsemen given the authority to do (v. 8)?

   [handwritten: kill 1/4 of the earth killed by famine, plague, wild beasts.]

4. Things have to be exposed before they can be dealt with. Things have to come to light before the surgeon can perform the operation. Ancient memories of guilt and sorrow must be raked up, however painfully, before they can be prayed through and healed. Revelation is, as it were, a cosmic version of the tough pastoral struggle over the deeply wounded soul. The soul of the world is aware of immediate problems and pains; but unless we look deeper, to the ancient patterns of conquest, violence, oppression and death itself we shall not begin to understand what needs to be done to be healed, really healed rather than merely patched over for a few more years.

What seems to be the ultimate goal of allowing the horsemen to ride into the world inflicting so much damage?

to allow things to get bad enough people will turn — plays up Egypt

5. For too long, over the last century at least, mainline Western churches have healed the wounds of the human race lightly, declaring "peace, peace" when there is no peace, except at the superficial level. How might we begin to look below the surface and help each other find deeper healing?

Peace requires confession, repentance, change in behavior

6. *Read Revelation 6:9-17.* Who does John see under the altar and what is their cry (vv. 9-10)?

Martyrs — sacrificed their lives / Avenge us

7. Why are they given white robes and told that they must wait a while longer (v. 11)?

So that more will die — martyrs — finite number of them

8. There is a long tradition, going back through the Psalms and the prophets to the children of Israel in Egypt, crying out to their God to do something at last (Exodus 2:23). This cry ("How long, O Lord, how long?") echoes down through the centuries, and is heard again as the fifth seal is opened. How is this cry echoed in our own day— in our families, churches and the world around us?

cries for relief, for justice, for peace.

9. What series of events does the sixth seal reveal? *Big events*

End of the earth
Sun turns black, moon turns red,
stars fall, mountain/islands removed.

Once again we must be careful about the symbolism. It is true that many in the ancient world saw eclipses, earthquakes, shooting stars and the like as signs and portents. John may be happy for people to hear those echoes. But in the Old Testament, language about the sun turning black and the moon becoming like blood, the stars falling from heaven, and so on, was regularly employed as a way of speaking about what we even today would call "earth-shattering events." By that phrase we wouldn't mean literally that "the planet broke in pieces." Likewise John did not at all mean actual earthquakes. By saying that, we would be referring to tumultuous events such as the fall of the Berlin Wall or the smashing of the Twin Towers on September 11, 2001: events for which it is hard to find appropriate language except through vivid symbol and metaphor.

10. Why are the kings of the earth, the rich and the powerful, singled out among all the people who hide in caves (vv. 15-16)?

They are powerless now, they cant stop these things from happening.

11. The thing those hiding are most afraid of is the combination of the Creator's gaze and the Lamb's wrath. Here there is, once more, a deep mystery. The phrase "the wrath of the Lamb" sounds like a contradiction in terms. Just as John has learned to see the Lion in terms of the Lamb, so the very notion of "wrath" is redefined by the fact that it is the Lamb's wrath.

Justice is on the way.

How does our view of "wrath" change when we realize that it belongs to the one who has embodied (in his own death) God's own self-giving, sacrificial love?

A long overdue reckoning

12. The only people who should be afraid of the Lamb's wrath are those who are determined to resist the call of love. In what ways might we respond to the call to love in the way of the Lamb in our lives?

PRAY

Hold in prayer all those throughout the world who are terrorized by war, famine, disease, poverty, persecution and injustices of all kinds. Cry out with those who suffer, "How long, sovereign Lord?" Then entrust them to the care of the God who is somehow present in the midst of all of these terrors, lovingly working to make all things new.

NOTE ON REVELATION 6

This is a good point to think about how the symbolism of chapters like this works. Obviously the four horsemen, and their riders, are symbols. John does not expect that his readers will shortly look out of the window and see these sinister characters riding by on the streets of Ephesus or Smyrna. But the sequence, too, is symbolic. John does not suppose that conquest is followed by violence and then by economic disaster and then by widespread death.

This is one of the differences between writing something with words and writing it with music. In music, you can have several lines which all happen at the same time, but with words you have to say everything in sequence. This sevenfold sequence is not chronological. It is an exposition of a sevenfold reality.

In the same way, we should not suppose that this sevenfold sequence of seals being opened is supposed to take place *before* the subsequent sequences of the trumpets (chapters 8–11) and the bowls of wrath (chapter 16). Rather, each of the sequences—and the material in between, too—is a fresh angle of vision on the same highly complex reality. If we look at the problems and pains of the world from *this* angle, God's answer is to draw out the arrogant wickedness of humans to its full extent and show that he is bringing his people safely through (chapter 7). If we look at those same problems and pains from the *next* angle of vision (chapters 8–11), God's answer is to allow the forces of destruction to do their worst, so that he can then establish his kingdom fully and finally over the world. And if we take a deep breath and begin the story again from yet a third angle of vision (chapters 12 and 13), we see the full depth and horror of the problem, to which God's answer will be to inflict on the rebellious world the equivalent of the plagues of Egypt, before finally rescuing his people and finally judging the dark powers that have for so long enslaved them (chapters 12–19).

7

SEALING GOD'S PEOPLE

Revelation 7

Sometimes you're in the middle of a nightmare which seems so real, so powerful and so horrible that when you wake up you can hardly dare to believe that it was only a dream, that the accident didn't happen, that so-and-so is still alive after all, that the monster attacking you was just in your imagination. Often it is difficult to tell which is dream and which is reality.

John is facing a similar problem with the little communities to whom he is sending this book. They are about to face a nightmare. Persecution is on the way, and they must be ready for it.

OPEN

Have you ever had a dream that felt so real you had a hard time convincing yourself it was just a dream? How did you respond?

Didn't want to go back to sleep.
✗ forget it ✗   - unempharped in experience

STUDY — *nothing for nnh*

1. *Read Revelation 7:1-8.* What are the angels at the four corners of the earth doing and why?

holding back judgment

2. The idea of "harming" the earth, the sea and the trees in verse 3 is harsh. This, we remind ourselves, is God's good creation, the natural order of which he said "very good" in Genesis 1 and from which, as we have seen, ceaseless praise arises before God's throne. Why, then, has the authority to harm God's creation been given to these angels?

> — *instruments of judgment.*
> — *earth — provides — life — can be taken away.*
> — *tree — birds ; Sea — everything included.*

3. The "seals" on a scroll were the kind of sticky wax whose purpose, in the ancient world and sometimes in the modern as well, was to keep important documents secure against prying eyes. You could always tell if the seal had been broken, since it would be stamped with the mark of the one who had sealed it up.

> — *not temporary —*

How does the term *seal* take on a new, though somewhat related, significance here (vv. 2-4)?

> — *seal is secure —*
> — *not going away —*
> — *permanent mark,*

4. Who makes up the 144,000 that John hears will be sealed (vv. 4-8)?

> *Dan is left out of the tribes listed here.*
> *Could be Martyrs.*
> *representation of the church.*

5. What benefit might the "seal" offer to those marked with it?

> — *security in salvation*
> — *belonging —*

6. *Read Revelation 7:9-17.* Who makes up the great multitude that John sees (v. 9), and how does this crowd seem to differ from those described in verses 4-8?

> *the church*

As with the Lion and the Lamb in chapter 5, we notice that in verse 4 John *hears* the number—144,000 broken down into 12 tribes—but then when he looks (v. 9) he *sees* the great, uncountable crowd. This strongly suggests that they are the same people, symbolically represented as the complete people of God (twelve thousand times twelve thousand), but actually consisting of a much larger number which nobody could count. And the people in this crowd, as we shall see, have not escaped suffering. They have come through it to safety on the other side, as Jesus himself passed through death to the immortal physical life of resurrection.

7. How does this passage help us understand how God is involved in our lives in the midst of great suffering or difficulty?

He's there. Keep eternity in view. No abandonment. Not home yet.

8. What is the response of the multitude to what God and the Lamb have done for them (vv. 14-15)?

Worship, praise,

9. What does it mean that God will "shelter" those gathered around him "with his presence" (v. 15)?

Comfort, order, peace

10. At this point, John glimpses the further future, the vision of the New Jerusalem itself (Revelation 21). In a wonderful role reversal the Lamb will turn into a shepherd, assuming the royal role of John 10 (the "good shepherd") and indeed the divine role of Psalm 23. This Lamb-turned-Shepherd guides the flock of his people to springs of living water (v. 17). What does this symbolize?

Gratefulness, thanksgiving, 21st Century

11. When in your life have you experienced God as Lamb or God as Shepherd?

Merciful, kind, blessed, how do we respond?

"We can't do anything" Resist that theology.

There hope - PRAY *- Generosity - Store house?*

Offer prayers for all who suffer, asking God to shelter them with his own presence and lead them safely through the danger. As you reflect on the image of Jesus as the slaughtered Lamb who is also the good Shepherd, give thanks that you are not being ruled by an uncaring king but by one who knows your suffering and is willing and able to guide you to the rivers of life. *Spiritual hunger & thirst.*

NOTE ON REVELATION 7:4-8

We should not suppose that this 144,000 consists of those ethnic Jews who are to be rescued. For John, the people of God now consists of all those, including of course the Jews who remain at the heart of the family, who believe in Jesus, who acknowledge him as Lord. Just as the New Jerusalem has the names of the twelve tribes of Israel inscribed on its gates, while the foundations have the names of the twelve apostles (Revelation 21:12-14), so here the twelve tribes do not indicate ethnic Jews over against a large crowd of Gentile Christians in verses 9-17— any more than the description of that great crowd in verses 14-17 in particular should be thought to apply to Gentile Christians only, not to Jewish followers of the Messiah. Rather, as always, John is using the rich symbolism of Israel's identity to mark out those who, through the Messiah, belong to God's renewed and rescued people, no matter what their ancestry.

8

THE GOLDEN CENSER
AND THE FIRST PLAGUES

Revelation 8

Bernard Levin was one of the greatest London journalists of the last generation. One of his many great loves was music. Levin relished the great moments of classical music, the operas of Mozart and Wagner in particular. He was no stranger to thunderous applause, standing ovations, the celebration of a delighted audience after a majestic performance. But on one occasion, at the end of a recital of Schubert songs by one of the finest singers of the day, he described how the audience simply sat in silence, and then, still in silence, got up slowly and left the concert hall. The spell of the music had been so powerful that nobody dared to break it with anything so mundane as clapping.

Such moments are precious and rare, and remind us, in our noise-soaked world, that silence can be not simply the absence of noise, a temporary and unwelcome piece of boredom, but a profound, still, deep experience in which one can sense aspects of reality which are normally drowned out by chatter and babble. That is the spirit in which we should hear what John has to say, that when the Lamb opened the seventh seal "there was silence in heaven, lasting about half an hour." A sense of awe, expectation and anticipation. The otherwise ceaseless praise of the four living creatures dies away. The song of the elders, the angels and the huge, countless crowd falls quiet. Everyone seems to be holding their breath. This, we sense, is the moment they've all been waiting for. We watch, hardly daring to breathe ourselves.

OPEN

Have you ever experienced a silence that seemed too meaningful to break? What made it so significant?

→ emotion-laden moments.

Silence **STUDY**

1. *Read Revelation 8:1-5.* What mood and feeling is created by these opening verses of chapter 8? *Something's about to start.* | *Expectation, anticipation, preparation*

   Throughout chapter 6 we watched, perhaps in dismay, as the Lamb removed the seals from the scroll which had been handed to him by the figure seated on the throne. The four horsemen; then the souls under the altar; then the terror seizing earth's inhabitants. Then there was a pause in chapter 7, with God's faithful people being sealed so that the great damage that was bound to be done upon earth when God's judgment came sweeping through would not harm them.

2. How does the pause of chapter 7, as we wait for the seventh seal finally to be opened in chapter 8, heighten the drama and add emphasis here?
   - calm before storm -
   - pause - then the big event.
   inevitable

3. Trumpets were used for various purposes in ancient Judaism, some-
    times in worship (especially at certain festivals) and, not unnatu-
    rally, in battle. One of the most celebrated of the latter occasions was
    when the Israelites circled Jericho and, at the blast of their trumpets,
    the walls fell down flat (Joshua 6). More generally trumpets were
    blown for warning, to sound the alarm.

    What role do you think the trumpets will play in this vision?

    Not subtle, getting   Attention, announcement → precursor

4. What is the role of the angel with the censer (vv. 3-5)?

    Justice, Judgment

5. We have already heard (in Revelation 5:8) that the prayers of God's
    people on earth are presented before God like incense. Now the angel
    approaches once more, and this time he is given a large quantity of
    incense. In some Jewish thinking, the praises of heaven must pause
    for a while so that the prayers of earth may be given a proper hearing.

    listen

    How does this picture of the prayers of the saints being offered up
    before the throne at this crucial moment challenge the way we think
    about prayer?

    *They are heard, and their
    numbers matter.*

6. *Read Revelation 8:6-13.* What do the first two trumpets bring (vv.
    6-9)?

    *hail, fire, blood
    mountain in the sea
    death / destruction 1/3*

7. The idea of a huge mountain being thrown into the sea is an image used by Jesus himself on occasion, for example, Mark 11:23, and was familiar in other Jewish writings of the time. Why is it significant that this vision uses symbols and ideas that were already familiar to John's readers?

[handwritten notes: Rule of 3? ; Credibility, understanding ; ring of familiarity.]

8. With these plagues, and continuing on into those which occur when the "bowls of wrath" are poured out in chapter 16, we are seeing a major rerun of the plagues with which God afflicted the Egyptians at the end of the Israelites' four hundred years of slavery. In Exodus 7–12 there are ten plagues, which strike both the people and the land, functioning as a warning to the Egyptians of the power of the God of Israel, and finally as the dramatic means by which, at Passover, Israel escapes (and then only because of the shed blood of the lamb).

The plagues which John now envisages would resonate, in the minds of his hearers, with the ancient Egyptian plagues, and assure them of the same result. We have already seen that Passover plays a significant part in the story John is telling. Indeed, the Lamb himself is who he is because he is the true Passover Lamb. We should not be surprised, then, that just as Egypt was smitten with plagues as both a warning and a means of liberation, so the whole world is to be smitten with similar plagues in order both to warn its inhabitants and to deliver God's people.

What plagues do the third and fourth trumpets bring (vv. 10-12)?

[handwritten notes: — poison water — darkness]

9. The picture of a giant star falling from the sky (v. 10) has resonances with the ancient story of a fallen angel being cast out of heaven (Isa-

iah 14:12). By including this detail, how might John be pointing us
to the ultimate meaning of what is being revealed in these plagues?

A final reckoning

10. Even after a century of war, terror and high-tech genocide, we are
still inclined, in the Western world at least, to pretend to ourselves
that the world has really become quite a pleasant place, with "evil"
merely a blip on the horizon which we can deal with easily enough.
However great the contrary evidence, this modern myth of the erad-
ication of evil through "enlightenment," leaving only a few minor
mopping-up operations (preferably in faraway places) before Utopia
finally arrives, has taken hold on popular imagination.

How does Revelation 8 underscore the seriousness of evil in our world?

Requires judgment, sweeping response

— hope → (evil is not going to triumph)

11. There is nothing wrong with being an earth-dweller. But the point
John is making, again and again, is that there are many who have
lived on earth as though there were no heaven, or as though, if
heaven there be, it was irrelevant. In what ways do we still see the
tendency to think this way in our own day?

— Living as if this is all there is
— Desperate measures —

12. How might we set a counter-example as those who do embrace God's
re-establishment of the rule of heaven on earth?

— [Responsibility] •

PRAY

Take a few minutes to sit in silence before the Lord in awe of all he has done and anticipation of what he will do. After this time of silence, commit the world into the care of God and ask that all might come to heed the warnings he has given and turn to him in repentance and love.

NOTE ON REVELATION 8:5

The "thunder, rumblings, lightning, and earthquake" come at the close of each section of the book of Revelation, picking up from their initial appearance in front of God's throne (4:5). They appear here at the close of the seven seals; at 11:19, after the seven trumpets have sounded; and at 16:18, once the seven bowls of wrath have been poured out. We are to understand that the commerce between heaven and earth, though vital for God's purpose and central to his eventual plan (21:1-8), will always be a matter of awe and wide-eyed wonder, and in the present time a matter for proper fear and trembling. God remains sovereign, and as long as earth remains the haunt of evil, his answer to it must be fire.

NOTE ON REVELATION 8:7-12

The stylized way in which the effects of the seven trumpets are described ought to remind us of what John's first readers certainly knew, that he wasn't actually talking about one-third of the earth, the seas and so on. He was talking about God's drastic action to purify the world, to cut it back as one would with a tree that had become dangerously diseased, removing the deadly cancer so that the rest may be saved. He was talking about the necessary work of radically upsetting the human systems by which millions had been enslaved and degraded, but which were kept in place by structures of apparent beauty, nobility and high culture. A little modification will not be enough. Only major surgery will do.

1/3 not literal – just a large share that is required.

9

LOCUSTS AND FIERY RIDERS

Revelation 9

It is already dark outside, and the wind is getting stronger. You are getting up to close the curtains when all the lights go out: a power failure. As you stumble your way to the cupboard by the back door in search of candles, you sense a cold wind coming at your face: the door is open! What's going on? Then you hear it: a low, growling, grinding sound, not far away. Grabbing a candle, you strike a match. The wind blows it out, but not before you catch a glimpse of Something just outside the door. Like a large dog, but . . . another match, you get the candle lit, but you wish you hadn't. It isn't a dog. It's—you don't know what it is. It's a monster! It's getting bigger! It's got huge teeth, enormous black wings, a long, spiky tail! You try to slam the door, but it's too late . . .

The stuff of horror movies, or nightmares, or both. We can only assume, when John wrote down this vision of the locusts, that he was intending to produce a similar effect. He lavishes more detailed description on these super-locusts than on any other creature in this vivid book.

OPEN

Do you watch horror movies? What attracts you to them or drives you away from them?

Unpleasant feelings.

STUDY

scared, afraid

1. *Read Revelation 9:1-12.* John's concept of the present creation includes a bottomless pit which, like a black hole in modern astrophysics, is a place of anti-creation, anti-matter, of destruction and chaos. What happens when the bottomless pit opens up (vv. 2-3)?

   Smoke, fire, oblivion
   furnace
   air, sun, darkened.

2. Why do you think John describes the super-locusts that emerge from the pit in so much detail (see vv. 7-10)?

   Shocking, frightening,
   VIVID,
   maybe we recognize them.

3. Humans were made to reflect their wise, loving Creator, but somehow their hearts have become full of rebellion, filth and wickedness. Now it appears that the same is true at a cosmic level. The world, though made by God and loved by God, has come to harbor within it such rebellion, such anti-creation destructiveness, that, though God normally requires it to be restrained, if it is to be dealt with it must, sooner or later, be allowed to come out, to show itself in its true colors.

   Crime, violence, persecution

   Where do we see evidence of this kind of widespread, cosmic harboring of rebellion and destructiveness in our own times?

   - conflict - WWI; WWII;

4. What are the limitations of the locusts' authority (vv. 4-5)?

Can't kill

warning - repentance.

5. The locusts' mission is not simply instant destruction. That would, it seems, be too kind. They are to torture people until they long to die but are unable to do so (v. 6). As with the plagues of Egypt, so we must assume that the aim here is to challenge the inhabitants of the earth to repent.

Why are such drastic measures sometimes needed in order to bring about repentance?

Confession - self-awareness

- acceptance /

6. We too have seen terrible things in our day such as using sophisticated military equipment to strike terror into human hearts. If we suppose that such destruction ultimately comes, like the insects-on-steroids in John's vision, from the bottomless pit, under the direction of Apollyon, what is our proper response?

repent - living as an example

7. *Read Revelation 9:13-21.* What happens when the sixth angel blows his trumpet (vv. 13-15)?

The ancient Israelites sometimes spoke of the great river Euphrates as their northeastern frontier. When the Romans swept through the

Middle East, sixty years or so before the birth of Jesus, the upper reaches of the Euphrates became their border too, against the legendary empire of Parthia, which stretched at its height across modern Iraq, Iran and Afghanistan as far as the Indus river in modern Pakistan. So when John sees in his vision four angels tied up by the Great River, the Euphrates, ready to be released and to lead their massive armies into battle, everyone from Jerusalem to Rome and beyond knew what this meant. Their worst political and military nightmares.

8. How are the riders and their horses described (vv. 17-19)?

fire, smoke, sulphur,

9. What do the horses and riders symbolize?

10. What is the response of the rest of humankind who are not killed by these plagues (vv. 20-21)?

Not repentant.

11. The final verses of chapter 9 indicate well enough the shape of John's understanding of the basic human plight. Like all mainline Jews of his day, he believed that human evil emerged from idolatry. You become like what you worship: so, if you worship that which is not God, you become something other than the image-bearing human being you were meant and made to be. Thus verses 20 and 21 stand in parallel. Worship idols—blind, deaf, lifeless things—and you become blind, deaf and lifeless yourself.

Promicous, abundance, more, acquireveness, security,

What are the idols that we are tempted to worship, and how do we become like them when we choose to serve them rather than God?

12. Repentance is a radical, heartfelt, gut-wrenching turning away from idols which promise delight but provide death. God longs for that kind of repentance. He will do anything, it seems, to coax it out of his rebellious but still image-bearing creatures.

How is God calling us to repent today?

PRAY

Grieve before the Lord over your own and all humankind's stubbornness and persistence in sin and rebellion. Offer prayers of confession and repentance. Pray for God's patience and mercy and ask that he would help you live to worship and serve him alone.

NOTE ON REVELATION 9:10-11

The "five months" for which the torture is to last probably reflects John's awareness that this was the normal life cycle, or at least period of activity, of a locust. But the underlying point is that their work here, though horrible, is limited.

The Hebrew word *Abaddon* means "the place of destruction," and the Greek word *Apollyon* means "destroyer," indicating the anti-creation energy here displayed.

10

A LITTLE SCROLL

Revelation 10

One of the most famous baseball umpires of all time, Bill Klem, earned his reputation by insisting that the umpire's word was not only final, but in a sense creative. On one celebrated occasion, he waited a long time to call a particular pitch. Some umpires would say that the ball thrown was, in its own right, either a "ball" or a "strike," either inside the strike zone or out. The umpire's ruling would merely be acknowledging the facts of the case. Klem was made of sterner stuff. "Well," asked the player, "is it a ball or a strike?"

"Sonny," replied Klem, "it ain't nothing 'til I call it."

Klem's belief in the power of his words may have annoyed both batters and pitchers in his time, but the idea of speaking words which create a new reality is an ancient one, finding classic expression in the great prophets. They are not only given visions or revelations of things that are to come. They are to speak words which somehow generate that new situation. The words, like God's own words, do things. "By the word of the Lord the heavens were made, and all their host by the breath of his mouth. . . . He spoke, and it came to be; he commanded, and it stood firm" (Psalm 33:6, 9). And when God puts words into the mouth of prophets, the same thing happens. This now puts John in the hot seat. There are new things yet to happen as part of God's purpose, *and John's words will bring them to pass.*

[handwritten margin notes: Our Words → Role in God's plan. | Involvement / Interpretation]

OPEN

How has the power of somebody's words affected your life or opened up possibilities that didn't seem to exist before?

[handwritten: – encouragement / – motivation / – try something new]

STUDY

[handwritten margin note: Back on our ...]

1. Read Revelation 10:1-11. How is the mighty angel described in verses 1-3?

[handwritten: Cloud, rainbow, pillar, sun / lots of light/color]

2. We've already seen, earlier in the book, several of the symbols mentioned in Revelation 10:1-3. We saw a cloud in 1:7, the sun in 1:16, a rainbow in Revelation 4:3 and a lion in 5:5. Look back at these passages. What clues do they give as to the significance of the angel described in 10:1?

[handwritten margin note: Big Deal]

[handwritten: God's appearance / constitutive elements / of universe – make life possible]

3. The angel also stands with one foot on the land and one on the sea. Taken together, what do they signify?

[handwritten margin note: The entire world / sphere]

[handwritten: Authority over earth – land & sea / Creative - Creation]

4. John is now given a little scroll and called to turn its words into prophecy which will bring God's purposes into reality. All this takes place as we are waiting with bated breath for the seventh trumpet to sound. Yes, says the angel, it is coming soon, and when it comes it will complete "God's mystery" (v. 7).

What is "God's mystery" that will be fulfilled in the days when the seventh trumpet is sounded?

[handwritten: Final Judgment – End of History]

5. The Lamb has removed the seals; now the scroll can be read. And
John is to be the one to do it. This, it seems, is the reason why he
was invited into the heavenly throne room. How is John invited to
participate in this (vv. 8-9)?

told to go and take the scroll and eat it

6. "Eating the scroll" is a vivid metaphor for the way in which the
prophet, then or indeed today, can only speak God's word insofar as
it has become part of the prophet's own life. It may be nourishing;
it may be bitter; it may be both. This is part of what it means to say
that God desires to act in the world through obedient human beings. Prophecy—speaking words which bring God's fresh order to
the world—is one special aspect of the larger human vocation, and
here John shoulders that responsibility.

Role

Must digest and love

Why is it important for us also to "eat" God's word before we speak
it to others?

Experience helps, familiarity, know the meaning, know the complexity.

7. How does God's word sometimes seem sweet to us and sometimes sour?

A combination of blessing and trial, easy to hear, harder to live.

8. What happens to the sweet-tasting scroll once it reaches John's
stomach, and what might this symbolize (v. 10)?

Difficulty in life living according to God's words and communicating them.

9. What in particular is John told that he must prophesy about (v. 11)?

Talk about the fate of many.

10. How might John have felt after receiving this commission?

[handwritten: Back or Earth]

[handwritten: Responsible, obligated, afraid. Given a mission - no turning back]

11. How, specifically, is God calling you to "eat" and speak his message today?

[handwritten: Get out the word]

*[handwritten:
- You are part of His plan
- You are called upon.
- You have a role.   Obedience]*

PRAY

Give thanks to God that he invites us to participate in his creative work by giving us words to speak his message. Openly express any fears or reservations you have about this vocation and ask that God might give you courage and strength to embrace this calling.

NOTE ON REVELATION 10:6

There will be no more time? This is not in the sense that "time shall be no more," leaving everything in the timeless "eternity" beloved of some nonbiblical philosophies. Rather the sense is that "time will have run out" for all those who are presuming on God's patience. Now things will reach their goal. This reminds us that the sequence of the seven trumpets is not meant to stand chronologically between the other "seven" sequences—the letters, the seals and the bowls—but is one key dimension of the same basic sequence. We are building up, at the end of chapter 11, to what could be the final climax of the book—except for the fact that we still have the entire second half of the book to come, in which the same story is approached from a radically different angle, spelling out in depth all sorts of aspects of the story which cannot be told until these preliminary tellings have done their work.

11

TWO WITNESSES
AND A SONG OF TRIUMPH

Revelation 11

People find many books puzzling, but the Bible is often the most puzzling of all. People find many parts of the Bible puzzling, but Revelation is often seen as the most puzzling book of all. And people find Revelation puzzling, but the first half of chapter 11—the passage now before us—is, for many, the most puzzling part of all. There are some other strong contenders for this dubious distinction, but chapter 11 can hold its own.

OPEN

What other books, chapters or stories of the Bible do you find puzzling or difficult?

Daniel, Isaiah, prophetic, symbolism

STUDY

when, conflicts;

1. *Read Revelation 11:1-14.* How is the tone of voice and the shape of the content of this passage different from what we have encountered so far in Revelation?

End is near, last gasp
Culmination — inevitability
Warning, conviction

2. What else does verse 1 say John is to measure besides the temple
   and the altar?

   Count worship[pers]

As is the case with an especially difficult passage like this one, many
have disagreed about its meaning. I am inclined to agree with those
who hold that John measuring the temple (which echoes similar prophetic actions in Ezekiel 40 and Zechariah 2) has nothing to do with
the Jerusalem temple, or with the heavenly temple/throne room of
chapters 4 and 5. By the time John was writing—indeed, this was
true from very early on in the Christian movement—the followers of
Jesus had come to see themselves as the true temple, the place where
God now lived through his powerful Spirit. So John's marking out
of this human temple, this community, is a way of signaling God's
solemn intention to honor and bless this people with his presence.

   believers   protection

3. What are the tasks of the two witnesses, and what do they have the
   authority to do (vv. 3-6)?

   Power to prophesy
   2 witness — churches

Why two witnesses? John has two great biblical stories in mind as
the backdrop. First, there is the story of Moses, who stood up to
Pharaoh, the pagan king of Egypt, and demonstrated God's power
with plagues including turning the Nile to blood (see v. 6 and Exodus 7:14–11:10). Second, there is the story of Elijah, who stood up to
Ahab, the paganizing king of Israel, and demonstrated God's power
by successfully praying for a drought and then by calling down fire
from heaven (see vv. 5-6 and 1 Kings 17:1 and 2 Kings 1:10).

   John doesn't mean, though some have thought this, that Moses
and Elijah would literally return to earth and carry out what chapter

11 says. That is to mistake the sort of writing this is. What John is saying is that the prophetic witness of the church, in the great tradition of Moses and Elijah, will perform powerful signs and thereby torment the surrounding unbelievers, but that the climax of their work will be their martyr-death at the hands of "the monster that comes up from the Abyss."

Church has influence/power.

4. Throughout the book of Revelation, the call of God's people is to bear faithful witness to Jesus, even though it will mean suffering, and quite possibly even shameful death. How is God calling us to bear faithful witness to Jesus today despite various obstacles?

power secularism, unbelief. Nihilism

5. If we understand the two witnesses to be symbolic for the whole of God's people, in what way might it be said that they "tormented those who live on earth"?

Convict unbelievers. can't enjoy your sins

6. What is the ultimate fate of the two witnesses (vv. 11-12)?

death, then, resurrection.

7. Why do the people remaining on earth suddenly "[glorify] the God of heaven" (v. 13)?

Finally see the truth, survivors see what is inescapable, inevitable.

8. When have you seen a dramatic event draw people to God?

9-11 ?

Billy Graham Crusades

9. *Read Revelation 11:15-19.* What happens when the seventh angel blows his trumpet?

New Kingdom is hailed.
Heaven & earth.

10. How will the kingdom of God look different than the kingdom of this world as we now know it?

Righteous, justice, all
things made right

11. Here we have a promise that God will put all things right. This is our great hope. How does this encourage you as you consider the specific people and situations for which you're currently praying about and trusting God?

Illness, poor judgment,
Conflict, strife,

PRAY

Join in the song of the twenty-four elders as they worship God:

Almighty Lord God, we give you our thanks,
Who Is and Who Was,
Because you have taken your power, your great power,
And begun to reign.

Give thanks to God that his kingdom is not only meant for heaven, but for our world too. Ask him to give you grace and strength to bear witness to his kingdom even in the midst of the chaos of life today.

NOTE ON REVELATION 11:2-3

Three-and-a-half years is a symbolic number. It is half of the *seven* which stands for completeness. Here it is broken down into the equivalent amount of 42 months or 1,260 days.

NOTE ON REVELATION 11:7-8

We haven't met this "monster" previously in Revelation. Nor have we yet discovered "the great city, which is spiritually called Sodom and Egypt, where their Lord was crucified." John will make all this clear in the several chapters that follow, where we learn that the "monster" is the might of pagan empire, presently embodied by Rome, and that the "city" is Rome itself, or maybe in this case the public world of the entire Roman Empire, which would include Jerusalem.

NOTE ON REVELATION 11:13

This verse is packed with powerful symbolism. When God judged Sodom and Gomorrah, he might have spared it if ten righteous persons were found there (Genesis 18:32). Now, however, only one-tenth of the wicked city is to fall, and nine-tenths is to be saved. When God was judging Israel through Elijah, only seven thousand were left who had not bowed the knee to the pagan god Baal (1 Kings 19:18). Now, however, it is only seven thousand who are killed, and the great majority are to be rescued. Suddenly, out of the smoke and fire of the earlier chapters, a vision is emerging: a vision of the creator God as the God of mercy, grieving over the rebellion and corruption of the world but determined to rescue and restore it, and doing so through the faithful death of the Lamb and, now, through the faithful death of the Lamb's prophetic followers.

12

THE WOMAN AND THE ANGRY DRAGON

Revelation 12

Ionce attended a memorial service for a famous sportsman, a cricketer who had been a boyhood hero for me and for many others. The church was packed, and a special place was reserved for other cricketers who had played with or against the great man and who had come to pay their respects. I was standing near the door when these other cricketers, a few dozen of them, walked in—and it was a very frustrating moment. Most of them, without a doubt, had also been household names. But for me and many others who were there, it was impossible to identify most of them. We remembered how they looked in their sporting prime, in their teens, twenties and thirties. Now, in their sixties, seventies and in some cases eighties, they were unrecognizable.

That problem of identification is, of course, the problem which we face in chapter after chapter of Revelation. We see these characters come and go across the pages. We know that there's a high probability that John intends them to represent, symbolically, some biblical theme or person, or (as in chapter 11) the corporate identity of God's people. But we wish he could have given them at least a little label, now and then, to give us a clue.

OPEN

Have you ever had difficulty identifying someone you thought you should know? Were there any clues that eventually helped you figure out who it was? *Clues — Reunions*

STUDY

1. *Read Revelation 12:1-6.* What two signs appear in heaven (vv. 1, 3)?

   Israel

   the church

2. What clue does John give us in verse 5 about the identity of the woman's child? (See also Psalm 2:9.)

   Savior

   Jesus

3. The dragon is a figure of considerable power. Why does he seek to devour the child?

   Make war with God

   Vengeful, enemy.

Some have suggested that the woman in the story is Mary, the mother of Jesus. But this is too hasty by far. That's not how this kind of symbolism works, and John tells us explicitly that she is a "sign," not a literal mother. It is far more likely she is a symbolic combination of two figures. First, there is Israel herself. She is here seen not as the faithless Israel rebuked so often by the prophets, but as the true, faithful Israel, the bride of Yahweh, the nation that had struggled to stay in God's path and follow his vocation.

The second image may well be Eve, the original mother of all human life. It is Eve, after all, who is told that her "seed" will crush the serpent's head (Genesis 3:15). The two identities go together. If the woman is "Israel," she is for that reason the one in whom God's purposes for humanity are to be realized. And that purpose includes, as a central and necessary part of the agenda, the crushing of the ultimate power of evil.

4. How are the mother and her child protected (vv. 5-6)?

Flee to the desert

5. How are God's people under attack from dark spiritual forces today?

Marginalize, persecution, discrimination, push Christianity away.

6. How does this vision help us to better understand where God is in the midst of the chaos and suffering that so often afflict his people?

God has a plan — He will triumph — long game.

7. *Read Revelation 12:7-18.* Who is involved in the war that breaks out in heaven (v. 7)?

Angels

8. John does not leave us guessing this time who the dragon is. He is clearly identified as the devil and the satan (literally, the accuser; see v. 10). What happens to the dragon and his angels after the war (vv. 8-9)?

Cast out of heaven, down to earth

9. If the war has taken place in heaven, why are the Lamb's people on earth given credit for the victory instead of Michael or God himself (v. 11)?

    they were in the struggle
    word of their testimony
    did not love their lives

10. What does the dragon do once he is thrown down to earth (vv. 13, 15)?

    made war against Israel,
    the Church.

11. The decisive battle has been won, and the devil knows it; but his basic nature of accuser is now driving him, more and more frantically, to the attack, to accuse where it's justified and where it isn't, to drag down, to slander, to vilify, to deny the truth of what the creator God and his son, the Lamb, have accomplished and are accomplishing.

    What spiritual accusations beset you, your Christian community or God's people as a whole today?

    Hypocrisy, bigoted, full of prejudice,
    intolerant, where haters
    Social death, career death, physical death

12. What hope and strength does this chapter give as we face those challenges?

    Expect it, It will happen.
    But it isn't the end.

PRAY ✳ *Death* ✳

Celebrate the decisive victory that has been won in heaven, praising God and the Lamb for conquering our ancient enemy. Offer prayers for all of God's people who continue to suffer under the frantic attacks of

the dragon, that they all may trust fully in God and find the strength
and endurance to overcome and thus participate in the victory that has
already been won for them.   *Strength and endurance*

NOTE ON REVELATION 12:6

The idea of the woman fleeing into the "wilderness" is probably yet
another reference to the exodus story, where the people of Israel escape
from the tyrant Pharaoh by going off into the desert, even though they
have fresh challenges to face once they get there. Once more, John is
telling a story in which his readers discover that they are not merely
spectators but actually participants. They are part of the "woman," part
of the family who are to be looked after even though, as we shall see, the
dragon is now pursuing them (v. 13).

13

TWO MONSTERS

Revelation 13

A parody is what you get when someone produces a fake which looks real but isn't. Sometimes this is done deliberately, for comic effect, as when people turn a Shakespeare tragedy like *Hamlet* into a short, funny skit, or play a Mozart symphony on kazoos and mouth organs. Sometimes it is done with the intent to deceive. And, if you deceive enough people, your parody becomes a new reality. That is what had happened across the ancient Near East in John's day.

The reality, as John and his readers knew not least from his vision in the throne room (chapters 4 and 5), was that the one sitting on the throne was the all-powerful, sovereign Lord of all creation. The parody, though, which was gaining ground all the time in western Turkey through the first century, was that the Roman Empire, gaining its ultimate authority from the satanic dragon, was putting itself about as the world ruler.

OPEN

What deception or cover-up do you recall that affected many people— on a personal, national or worldwide scale?

Holocaust

STUDY

1. *Read Revelation 13:1-10.* What does John see rising out of the sea next to the dragon and how does he describe it (vv. 1-2)?

2. This passage draws heavily on a section from the Old Testament that was hugely popular in the first century. Read Daniel 7:2-8. What similarities and differences do you see between Daniel 7 and Revelation 13?

3. The ultimate powers of the spiritual world prefer not to show themselves, but to act through others. They choose secondary or tertiary intermediaries; they give them some of their power; they back them up where necessary. We are today perhaps more aware than some of our forebears of how what we call "dark forces" go to work.

   What are some of the agents that do the dirty work of the dark forces in our world?

   Agents – crime, fraud, corruption false leaders.

4. In verses 3-4, how do the inhabitants of the earth respond to the monster (or "the beast," as some translations put it)?

   Worship, follow joy,

5. Why does the monster make life miserable for the people of God (vv. 5-8)?

6. The last verse of this section may reflect John's sober realism when contemplating the scene he has now drawn. Some people are going to be taken captive. Others are going to be killed with the sword. That's just the way it is. John says in verse 10 that our proper response to this harsh reality is to be patient and have faith. What does it look like to live this way in such circumstances?

Realistic — pre-destined, plan — be patient.

7. *Read Revelation 13:11-18.* How does the second monster differ from the first one?

Seems gentle, but speaks like a dragon

Propaganda minister

8. Why might John note the detail that this monster has "two horns like those of a lamb" (v. 11)?

looks harmless.

9. The second monster, like the first but subordinate, seems to be the local elites, in city after city and province after province, who do their best not only to copy the monster at a local level but insist, in order to keep the monster's favor, that everybody in their domain should worship the monster.

In what ways are national and local governments sometimes responsible for perpetuating evil rather than helping to overcome it?

leave bad people in place, encouraging disorder, lawlessness

10. Why does the second monster require everyone to be "marked" (vv. 16-17)?

Uneven administration of justice — Marked — Approved, license,

11. For Christians at the time John wrote Revelation, worshiping or not worshiping the Roman powers was quickly becoming the dividing line between people who were acceptable in the community and people who weren't. Not long after this time, some local officials introduced a formal requirement that unless you had offered the required sacrifices you weren't allowed in the market. From quite early on the Christians were faced with a stark alternative: stay true to the Lamb and risk losing your livelihood, the ability to sell or buy; or capitulate to the monster, sacrifice to Caesar at the behest of the local officials, and then everything will be all right—except your integrity as one of the Lamb's followers.

We can understand the dilemma faced by those Christians back then. We like to think that we would always choose the reality and reject the parody. How are we tempted to compromise our faith in order to make life easier?

Hide your light under a bushel
lonely to be different.

12. What can we do now so that, when we face even more serious situations, we respond well?

do a good job. — Try to
excel at what you do.

PRAY

In light of the immense power of the monster to deceive us and manipulate us into worshiping it rather than the Lamb, pray urgently. For wisdom, courage and endurance for ourselves and all of God's people throughout the world. Pray also for rulers and governments, that they might not be co-conspirators with the monster but rather seek to guide their people with goodness and justice in the way of the Lamb.

NOTE ON REVELATION 13:3

The year after the death of the brutish Roman emperor Nero (in A.D. 69) must have looked like a mortal wound to the whole monstrous Roman system. But rumors went around that Nero hadn't died after all—or that he had indeed died, but had then come back to life. Several would-be "Nero-alive-again" leaders emerged, and, though none lasted long, the rumor persisted.

NOTE ON REVELATION 13:4

What is John getting at when he says people worshiped the dragon and the monster? One emperor after another of the era had his image on coins inscribed with the words "son of god." They also would dress up in the garb traditionally associated with this or that ancient pagan divinity. And once the emperor becomes a god, there is no room for other gods. It's all right if local and tribal deities are still worshiped, so long as one worships the new god, Rome and the emperor. But if one refuses— as the Christians knew they were bound to refuse—then a collision course is set (v. 15).

NOTE ON REVELATION 13:18

The final verse of the chapter is one of the most famous in the whole book. It offers the greatest parody of all. It is more or less certain that the number 666 represents, by one of many formulae well known at the time, the name *Nero Caesar* when written in Hebrew characters. (Many peoples, and many languages, used letters as numbers, as we would if we devised a system where A=1, B=2 and so on.) The monster who was, is not, and is to come looks pretty certainly to be Nero.

But the number 666 isn't just a cryptogram. It's also a parody. The number of perfection would be 777. For John there is little doubt that Nero, and the system he represented and embodied, was but a parody of the real thing, one short of the right number three times over. Jesus was the reality; Nero, just a dangerous, blasphemous copy.

THE LAMB'S
ELITE WARRIORS

Revelation 14:1-13

On the hill in the distance I could see the little procession, tiny but silhouetted against the sky in the bright Middle-Eastern evening. In my country the sheep are brought from one field to another by people with sticks and dogs. In the Middle East, to this day, the shepherd goes on ahead and the sheep follow him or her. They know the shepherd's voice, but they also know that they can trust him or her to lead them to pasture, to water, to safety. No sticks, or dogs, are required.

Jesus himself, of course, used this image of the shepherd in the tenth chapter of John's Gospel. And his call to people to "follow him" is one of the most persistent commands he ever issued. One might almost say that, in the Gospels, "following Jesus" is the basic phrase which describes someone who belongs to Jesus, who believes in him (e.g., Matthew 4:19; 8:22; 9:9, etc.). But, in John's Gospel particularly, we find some poignant and striking passages on this theme. "If anyone serves me, they must follow me," he said (John 12:26). Peter insists that he will follow Jesus absolutely anywhere, to prison or even to death (John 13:37; Luke 22:33), but Jesus solemnly warns him that he will in fact deny that he even knows him.

All that is in the background as we find, in this definition of the Lamb's elite warriors, the sentence: "They follow the lamb wherever he goes" (v. 4).

OPEN

What makes you trust someone enough to follow him or her? Does this come easily to you or is it a struggle?

STUDY

1. *Read Revelation 14:1-5.* Who are the people gathered around the Lamb on Mount Zion (v. 1), and where have we seen them before in this book?

   144,000 — Chap 7 — earliest Jewish.
   Jewish? converts, believers believers.

2. Why do they have God's name written on their forehead?

   — Sealed — being a priority
   not being ashamed

3. Why is this crowd said to be "first fruits" for God and the Lamb?

   loyalty
   committed, - top priority.

4. If we are likewise to follow the Lamb wherever he goes, we first need to answer, Where is he going? How would you answer that?

   Christ follower.
   not idol worshipers

5. The closer we are to God and to his Lamb, the more we see everything clearly and should speak everything truthfully. The satan does his best work by keeping things out of people's minds altogether. Where that fails, he persuades them to believe, and to pass on, lies. Following the Lamb means rejecting the lie.

   telling yourself the truth.

What lies about God and the world does the accuser tell you?

6. How might we resist these lies and follow the Lamb in truth and faithfulness?

Rewards to come.

7. *Read Revelation 14:6-13.* What is the "eternal gospel," the good news that the first angel announces to all the people of earth in verses 6-7?

8. Babylon, the capital of the great empire that swallowed up the remaining Israelite tribes in 597 B.C., was the city that remained ever after in the Jewish memory as the paradigm of wickedness, of idolatry, immorality and sheer cruelty.

How does the spirit of Babylon still seem to live on in our own day?

It's not going to be ok for unbelievers.

9. What judgment does the third angel pronounce on those who are implicated in the monstrous evil of "Babylon" (vv. 9-11)?

No rest —

— Hell looks bad —

10. What is found in this judgment can only be heard with awe, and with the recognition that the deep seduction of evil really can swallow people up whole. John is eager, anxiously eager, to prevent any

of Jesus' followers being sucked down into that dark whirlpool of wrath. What do these warnings show us about the character of God?

11. Why are those who "die in the Lord" said to be "blessed" (v. 13)?

Satisfaction, rest from labor, capacity to enjoy heaven

12. What does it look like for us to follow Jesus (v. 12) even in the face of such difficult warnings of impending judgment?

Warnings — final appeal — End of the Bible →

PRAY

As you celebrate with those who follow the Lamb and share in his victory, offer up prayers for your community of faith and for all believers everywhere. Pray that you all would endure and hold fast to Jesus to the end as you labor here on earth to make that victory known. As you consider the difficult warnings given to those who are caught up in the worship of the monster, offer prayers for all those who have been deceived by this world's evil systems. Pray that they might repent and turn away from the monster to follow the Lamb.

NOTE ON REVELATION 14:4

Ancient Israel had a clear policy about going to war; if war was justified, war was also holy, and those who fought in it had to obey special rules of purity, including abstention (for the time) from sexual relations (see, for example, Deuteronomy 23:9-10; 1 Samuel 21:5). As usual, we need to be clear about the symbol and the reality to which it points. In the symbol,

clear choice — A battle lines are drawn

this body consists of 144,000 (we have met them before, of course, in chapter 7); they are in fact a great company which nobody could count. They are, in other words, the ideal representatives of the people of God, permanently ready for battle.

This great crowd, surrounding the Lamb, is not the sum total of all believers. It is the beginning, the great advance sign of an even greater harvest to come. That is the point of the "first fruits" image in verse 4. At the ancient Jewish harvest time, the first sheaf of wheat (or whichever crop it might be) was offered to God as the "first fruits," signifying the expectation and prayer that there would be much more on the way. Even so, these 144,000 are to be an encouragement to the churches. Already there is a great multitude! The Lamb is winning the victory! We can carry on patiently.

NOTE ON REVELATION 14:8

Babylon is used as a symbol later in Revelation 16, 17 and 18, where John clearly means "Rome." He is seeing Rome through the lens, in particular, of Babylon as presented by two of the greatest Old Testament prophets.

The first is Isaiah. In chapters 40–55 the Israelites in exile have almost given up hope. Babylon, where they have been taken in exile, seems so great and all-powerful. Yet God will rescue his people, re-establish the covenant and renew the whole creation. In that context the prophet announces the arrival of a herald with "good news" (52:7)—just as John tells us here that he sees an angel carrying "an eternal gospel." What is this good news? First, "Your God reigns!" (52:7, 9). Second, "Your God is coming back!" (52:8; 40:5). Third, "God is doing a powerful and public work of rescue!" (52:10).

The other passage comes from Jeremiah, who seems to have spent most of his life in the terror and horror of the Babylonian invasion and its aftermath, the sorrow of exile. In chapter 50, he begins two long chapters of sustained condemnation of Babylon. And now at last we can, perhaps, begin to understand also why Revelation 14 says what it does.

REAPING THE HARVEST AND
PREPARING THE PLAGUES

Revelation 14:14–15:8

Imagine a village in the outlying countryside of ancient Judaea. It's a long way from the city, and even traders don't come there that often, far less government officials. A circuit judge comes to the neighboring small town once every few months if they're lucky. But that doesn't mean that nothing needs doing. A builder is cheated by a customer, who refuses to admit his fault. A widow has her small purse stolen, and since she has nobody to plead for her, she can do nothing. A family is evicted from their home by a landlord who thinks he can get more rent from someone else. And a con artist has accused a work colleague of cheating him, and though nothing has been done about it the other workers seem inclined to believe the charge. And so on. Nobody can do anything about any of these—until the judge comes and justice is handed down.

When he comes, expectations will be massive. Months of pent-up frustrations will boil over. The judge will have to keep order. He will have to hear each case properly and fairly, taking especial care for those with nobody to speak up for them. And then he will *decide*. Judgment will be done. Chaos will be averted and order will be restored. The cheats will be put in their place, the thief punished and made to restore

Pervasive injustice.

the purse. The village as a whole will heave a sigh of relief. Justice has
been done.

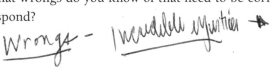

OPEN

What wrongs do you know of that need to be corrected? How will you
respond?

STUDY

1. *Read Revelation 14:14-20.* What's the meaning of the symbols mentioned in verse 14 that are used to describe the one like the Son of
   Man?

2. Verse 20 offers a horrible sight of blood flowing out of the winepress,
   "as high as a horse's bridle, for about two hundred miles." The passage is often read as the story of great and terrifying judgment, with
   Jesus himself executing God's wrath with his sickle (vv. 14-16), and
   an angel from heaven gathering up the "grapes of wrath," understood as the wicked nations who are about to suffer God's eternal
   anger. But the harvest imagery, and the natural implications it would
   carry, tell strongly against this. The previous chapter has warned
   God's people against worshiping the monster; the next chapter will
   see those same people, with victory won, singing the new song by
   the sea of glass. How have they come from the one place to the other?
   By, it seems, being themselves the harvest, the vintage, of the Lord.
   These are images of salvation, not of condemnation.

   With this image of salvation-through-suffering, John is encouraging his readers to face the prospect of persecution in faith and patience. The whole passage is designed to convey a powerful message

which we need today as much as ever. God's time will come; God will bring his people safely home.

> What if, in the face of the great evil and injustice that millions have faced in history, God did no more than say, "There, there. Boys will be boys"? What would be the reaction of the victims of that evil?

No sense of justice —
is God really good?

3. How then might we say that judgment is good?

Makes the losses and
suffering worth something.

4. God will take even the wickedness and rebellion of the world and make it turn to his praise and to the salvation of his people. How does this message bring you hope today?

honesty, justice is important.
victims —

5. *Read Revelation 15.* What is significant about the seven plagues the angels bring (v. 1)?

Justice is a promise

6. Whose song do the martyrs sing (v. 3)?

7. What are the "judgments" of God mentioned in verse 4 that have

been revealed in Revelation, and how do they draw the nations in to
worship the Lamb?

8. How might we explain God's judgments in a way that will draw
    people to the Lamb?

    People need to believe in ultimate justice.

9. The song of 15:3-4 is called a song of Moses. This recalls God's
    great act of judgment on Egypt and salvation for Israel when Mo-
    ses brought Israel through the Red Sea. Likewise the martyrs, those
    who have "won the victory over the monster and over its image, and
    over the number of its name" (v. 2), have discovered that they have
    come through death to life.

    What happens in the temple after the angels are given the bowls of
    wrath (vv. 7-8)?

10. The reference in verse 8 to no one being able to enter the heavenly
    temple is reminiscent of 1 Kings 8:10-11 during the dedication of
    Solomon's temple: "When the priests withdrew from the Holy Place,
    the cloud filled the temple of the LORD. And the priests could not
    perform their service because of the cloud, for the glory of the LORD
    filled his temple." How does this help us understand what is going
    on in 15:8?

11. How do we see ourselves differently when we pause to consider God's immense power, glory and the reasons why he executes judgment on the earth?

PRAY

Offer up the song the martyrs sing, glorifying the name of God for his great works, his holiness and his just judgments. Give thanks that even the nations will see God's greatness and come to worship before him. Pray for all those who follow the Lamb as they endure the violent reaping process and ask that God will bring them home rejoicing when the harvest is complete.

NOTE ON REVELATION 14:20

When speaking of the two-hundred-mile-long river of blood, we must once again remind ourselves that we are reading a symbolic prophecy, not a literal one. The idea of something flowing away from a city, and being measured for depth, carries a distant memory of the water of life which flows from the city at the end of Ezekiel (47:1-12). It may be that John, with his visionary imagination working overtime, sees the swelling river of blood as playing a similar role, though whether it will be to effect a further work of grace or a further work of judgment we cannot easily say. Of course at the end of Revelation (22:1-6) we also see a river flowing out of the city. This one, as in Ezekiel, is of the water of life.

That's how much justice is due

THE SEVEN PLAGUES

Revelation 16

The lunch had been substantial, the meeting was tedious, the room was warm and the speakers droned on and on. The chairman noticed that one of his colleagues was finally subsiding into slumber. With cruel timing, he waited until the poor man's head had come to rest on his arms, folded on the table in front of him. Then, interrupting the speaker, he said, "Perhaps Dr. Johnson would like to give us his opinion on this matter?"

We all looked at our colleague, by now happily asleep. His neighbor dug him in the ribs. Pulled back out of his dream, he had no idea that he had been asked a question, let alone what it was about.

That's the kind of shock that John administers to his hearers in verse 15. Suddenly, in the midst of the terrible last three plague-oracles, he turns to them and says, "Hey! Stay awake at the back, there! Jesus is on the way, and you don't want to be caught half naked, do you?"

OPEN

Have you ever unintentionally fallen asleep somewhere in public? How were you awakened?

STUDY

1. *Read Revelation 16:1-9.* What are each of the four bowls of wrath poured out on and what do they have in common?

   1. Sores   2. sea blood

   3. rivers blood. 4. Scorching sun
       springs blood.   5. Railway

2. What, then, are the implications and significance of these four bowls?

   Are they literal?

   6. Euphrates dries up

   7. earthquake
       hailstones

3. Why does the "angel of the waters" burst out in praise when the third bowl of wrath is poured out on the rivers and springs (vv. 4-6)?

   Celebrating judgment.

4. The "wrath" of the creator God consists of two things, principally. First, he allows human wickedness to work itself out, to reap its own destruction. Second, he steps in more directly to stop it, to call "time" on it, when it's got out of hand. If we knew our business, we would thank God for both of these, even though both can appear harsh. They need to be. If they were any less than harsh, the wickedness in question would merely pause, furrow its brow for a moment and then carry on as before.

   wickedness reaps its own destruction.

   How do we see a mixture of both these types of wrath in these first four bowls or plagues?

   Bring destruction on ourselves.

5. What we are faced with in this chapter is neither a capricious or ill-tempered divine being nor a careless, laissez-faire world ruler. We

are faced with the God who made the world, and whose generous love is seen most clearly in the sacrifice of his own son, the Lamb, the one who shares his very throne.

How does the picture of God we find in this chapter reshape the way we understand the nature of "love" and our idea of how God extends his love to us?

— Judgment is celebrated.
— We need judgment.

6.   *Read Revelation 16:10-21. What is the target of the fifth plague?*

Throne of the beast
kingdom falls in darkness

Those who fall under judgment here are those who have been given every chance to repent, and have refused. They have chosen to go down with the monsters rather than to suffer and be vindicated with the Lamb.   *Refused to repent*

7.   The sixth plague awakens again, as in Revelation 9, the deep-seated fear in John's society about the great enemy to the east, in their case Parthia. The Euphrates River formed the boundary, and like the river Rhine in Europe was a natural barrier relatively easy to defend. But the sixth angel's bowl, when poured out, dries up the river, so as to prepare the way for a very different kind of exodus: instead of the children of Israel going dry shod through the Red Sea, the kings from the east can now charge with their armies across the river, ready to attack.

Why are the kings of the earth drawn into such a foolish confrontation (vv. 13-14)?

Spirits have stirred them up against believers, against God,

8. Why does John suddenly issue an encouragement to his readers to "stay awake" (v. 15)?

Be alert - wake up -

9. How do we also need to "wake up" to what is happening around us in the world?

Be ready for Christ's return.

10. Why does the voice from the throne announce "It is done!" after the seventh bowl of wrath is poured out (v. 17)?

earthquake, hail.

11. The vision of the seventh plague (vv. 17-21) does not reveal the collapse of the physical earth. John's hearers would have no difficulty in getting the point since the prophets used the same sort of metaphorical language to describe God's judgment on the nations in their day, not the literal end of the planet which obviously didn't happen back then (see Isaiah 24, for example). Terrible things will happen in human society, for which the only fitting metaphor will be earthquakes and huge hailstones. This is the only way to describe the collapse of the entire social and political system *on* the earth.

As we consider this news of the impending collapse of the world's idolatrous systems—its economic, social, environmental and political systems—what does it mean to be faithful in the present?

All these systems will fail. Remember the long term result.

PRAY

With the angel of the waters in this chapter, give thanks to God for being the righteous judge of the earth and not allowing injustice to prevail forever. Pray that you—along with all the followers of the Lamb—may stay awake and alert so as not to be deceived by the dragon and the monstrous systems of the world which are doomed to complete destruction.

NOTE ON REVELATION 16

As with the seals and the trumpets, the first four bowls seem to belong to one set, and the last three to another. Unlike the seals and the trumpets, however, there is no gap, no pause, between the sixth and the seventh, just as there is no chance, now, of further time for repentance. Nonetheless, as mentioned above, in verse 15 John wants to make sure we are not lulled into complacency. It is a serious danger that deceitful spirits be let loose into the world. Be alert. Keep awake. Stay faithful.

As said previously, this chapter does not describe things that must happen *before* the events of chapters 17–20 take place. As with the three sequences of seven, these are different angles of vision on the same ultimate reality. As the voice from the temple declares in verse 17: "It is done!" It's happened. It's been completed.

NOTE ON REVELATION 16:16

Armageddon is literally "Mount Megiddo." In biblical times there was a town called Megiddo (which still exists today), some way inland from Mount Carmel in the north of Palestine, where several major battles took place in ancient times. Though no Mount Megiddo as such is known in ancient Israel the area was a well-known battlefield, and the town of Megiddo was close to mountains where, in prophetic symbolism, such conflicts might occur. It would, in any case, be most unusual for John suddenly to use a place name literally, and we should not suppose he has done so here. His point is simply that all the powers of evil must be brought to one place, so that they can be dealt with there. This is why the three frogs are allowed to perform their deceits.

THE MONSTER
AND THE WHORE

Revelation 17

I remember my excitement when, as a boy, I learned to read a map. Someone had given me a "maps made easy" sort of book, which explained how all the symbols worked. I remember being especially fascinated by the contour lines. Growing up as I did in a part of the country with plenty of hills to climb, I loved to imagine the gentle slopes with spaced-out contours and the steep or even sheer sides of the hill where the contours were so close together that there seemed no space, and sometimes indeed was no space, between them. And then there were the forests, the churches, the post offices and so on, all picked out with their own little symbols. Now, of course, you can go online and switch to and fro from a traditional style of map to an aerial photograph, and back again. That makes it easy, though no less fun. But the need for symbolic designs has not gone away. And the need to be able to interpret them remains.

Of course, if someone climbing a hill were to object that there were no contour lines on the hill itself, we would explain that these were merely mapmakers' symbols to tell you something about the reality, not actual representations of what you'd find when you got there. I doubt if anyone actually does make that mistake, but people frequently make the equivalent mistake when faced with a bit of apocalyptic "decoding" such as we find in the present passage. John has already given us a symbolic picture of the monster and the whore. Now he's going to tell us—unusually for him—what it all means, step by step. But will it work? Will we be able to see, as it were, the contour lines when we get to them?

OPEN

Do you enjoy working puzzles, decoding symbols or deciphering codes? Why or why not?

M Ap –

STUDY

1. *Read Revelation 17:1-8.* Whose judgment does the angel invite John to observe next?

    Roman Empire

2. Why is the image of the "whore" used to describe Babylon and the system it represents?

    for sale, no principles

    — Sell out — license –

3. This terrifying, multilayered denunciation of the outwardly delightful and inwardly deceitful city ought to give pause for serious thought to all those of us who live within today's glossy Western culture— and all others who look on and see our glitzy world from afar.

    Where are we in this picture?

4. Babylon has worshiped idols: the quick-fix pseudo-divinities that promise the earth, take all you have to give and then leave you with nothing. What are the life-draining effects of serving false gods today?

False hope — politics, riches, gambling, sports, leaders, debt & credit, possessions,

5. What does it mean that the whore has become drunk with the blood of God's people (v. 6)?

killing them, killing believers

6. What does it mean that the monster "carries" the whore of Babylon and gives her power (vv. 7-8)?

Clears away the underbrush — just likes resentful, destruction, hatred, misery.

7. *Read Revelation 17:9-18.* What explanation does the angel offer for the identity of the seven heads and ten horns first mentioned in verse 7?

Rome — Emperors. Paganism

8. What do the ten kings do first in verses 12-14?

Make war against believers.

9. In what way might we describe the next action of the ten kings (vv. 15-18) as "poetic justice"?

They go down evil destroys itself —

10. What examples can you think of in which evil ended up destroying itself recently?

Sit back and watch

Evil destroys itself.

11. What encouragement and hope do you find in this chapter and why?

Evil has limits, not triumphant

God wins in the end.

12. The abiding and overriding lesson for the church, then and now, should be clear. The brutal but seductive "civilizations" and national empires, which ensnare the world by promising luxury and delivering slavery, gain their power from the monster, the System of Imperial Power. Some have called this "the domination system," a system which transcends geographical and historical limitations and reappears again and again in every century. John's readers already know that this system itself gains its power from the dragon, the accuser, the satan.

How might we help those who suffer under the afflictions of the world's systems?

PRAY

Offer prayers for all who are afflicted by the abominations of Babylon, those who are oppressed by poverty, violence and injustice of every kind. Pray that you and all the followers of the Lamb would find strength and courage to resist the whore's seductive powers. Give thanks to God that

in his great wisdom, he will allow the evil systems to run their course
and ultimately meet their final end.

NOTE ON REVELATION 17:5

One of the great images in the Old Testament is that of Israel as Yahweh's bride, and one of the saddest prophetic images for when that relationship goes wrong is Hosea's picture, based on his own tragic experience of marriage, of Israel playing the whore and going off after idols.
This is probably the root of John's particular vision. Likewise "Babylon"
has worshiped idols. Babylon was an empire that had ended centuries
before John wrote. So his readers would have known this was code for
the Roman Empire.

NOTE ON REVELATION 17:9-18

What do the seven heads and ten horns on the monster (first mentioned
in 17:3) represent? John's first clue is straightforward: "The seven heads
are seven hills, on which the woman sits." No problem: there really are
seven hills in Rome (I've been up them), and everybody in the ancient
world who knew anything about Rome knew that this was so. The seven
kings may represent the seven Roman emperors from Augustus to Otho
during whose reign John may have been writing. (Nero was fifth.) But
more likely the kings are symbolic, *seven* representing perfection. The
seven kings then stand for the apparent perfection of the monstrous kingdom, with the eighth (though one of the seven) a king who will appear
to take the kingdom forward into a new day, but who will instead lead
it to its destruction. John is saying the monster's kingdom looks perfect
and impregnable, but forces from within its own ranks will destroy it.
It is likely that the additional "ten kings" are also part of the monstrous
system, different ruling elites within the larger Roman Empire.

Babylon is symbolic —

Really - Rome

Babylon's Judgment

Revelation 18

We smelt it before we saw it: a sour, bitter stench which seemed to cling to the nostrils. We looked at one another and ran outside. There, about a mile away, but with a gentle wind carrying it in our direction, was a cloud of thick, gray-black smoke, rising above the trees, hanging in mid-air. As we listened, we could even hear the noise of crackling. Soon a crowd gathered. It was the old mill at the bottom of the road. Still half-full of bales of wool, it had caught light. Soon, on that bright Friday morning, it was beyond rescue. For days afterwards, despite the fire brigade's energetic hosing, there were still smouldering remnants, the sour smell still in the air.

Now magnify a mill in a country lane by a million, and instead of an old woollen mill imagine a city with every kind of building and every kind of trade. Suddenly, in an hour, it is all gone. Those who remember one or other of the great stock market crashes will know that sense: systems that you could, literally, bank on suddenly collapsed. The bottom goes out of the market. Millionaires become paupers overnight. The speed of ruin is crucial to the sense of shock in the haunting description found in Revelation 18.

OPEN

When have you experienced a sudden, dramatic change that greatly impacted your life? *— Life changing —*

STUDY

1. *Read Revelation 18:1-8.* What message does the angel with great authority bring (vv. 2-3)?

   Judgment on Babylon

2. As those who live in a society that places a high value on human achievement, what lessons might we learn from the fall of Babylon?

   Human achievement can be turned to wicked ends.

3. Babylon is the city which tried, like Babel of old, to make itself The Place, the summit of human achievement, by its own efforts and to its own glory—and which ends up shrinking to a shell, with the wild desert creeping back into its palaces, its temples, its fine streets and shops and courtyards. Creation will reclaim what arrogant humans had thought to construct.

   The angel who shouts out that Babylon has fallen (echoing Isaiah 21:9 and Jeremiah 51:8) is bringing the news that human arrogance and oppression, and the wanton luxury and vice to which they lead, will not have the last word. God will have the last word, and creation itself will hear this word as a word of freedom, a sigh of relief, a flood of glorious light (v. 1) let in upon a darkened dungeon.

   What specific judgments are pronounced on Babylon for her sin (vv. 6-8)?

   Human achievements don't amount to much don't save you

4. How is this a just punishment for Babylon?

- judgment -

—total paganism —

5. Structures of authority are part of the good creation (Colossians 1:15-16). The problem comes when those structures assume powers beyond those of being humble servants of God's good purposes for his world and his image-bearing creatures.

    How do we discern the point at which a government or other worldly power passes from being a servant of God to putting itself in the place of God? *Who / What do we trust?*
    Servant

    — gov't expecting too much

6. In what ways do we also need to "come out" from present-day "Babylons" with their corrupt systems, and separate ourselves from their ways? *Separate ourselves —*
1st John 2 — Do not love the world.

7. *Read Revelation 18:9-24.* How do the kings and merchants of the earth react to the fall of Babylon (vv. 9-11)?
Do not lay up
Treasures on earth

8. In verses 12-13, John builds up a marvelous catalog of luxury goods as well as the basics of trade—flour, wheat, cattle and so on. But what horror do we find at the end of this list?

9. John does not say that the gold, silver, precious stones and the rest
   were bad things which nobody should have celebrated in the first
   place. Interestingly, many of them find an honored place in the
   New Jerusalem of Revelation 21. Rome was able to bring all these
   fine commodities, listed in verses 12-14, from the ends of the earth.
   Among the things John mentions are goods that would have come
   from India, China and Africa, as well as Arabia, Armenia and beyond. This was truly a worldwide trade.

   But when you "worship" these things—give them a place of prom-
   inence only due God—they become idols. And we can tell when this
   point is reached because idols demand sacrifices. When you worship Mammon the money-god (or Mars the war-god, or Aphrodite
   the sex-goddess), they will demand sacrifices all right. And some
   of those sacrifices will be human. The giveaway point comes at the
   end of verse 13. Here, in the middle of this lament over Babylon, we
   find one of the many places in the New Testament where a small but
   significant note of implacable protest is raised against the entire system upon which the ancient world was built. Slavery—the buying,
   selling, using and abusing of human beings as though they were on a
   par with gold and silver, ivory and marble (except that you could ill-
   treat them in a way you would never do with your luxury jewels and
   furnishings!)—was the dark thread that ran through everything
   else. Slavery was to the ancient world, more or less, what steam, oil,
   gas, electricity and nuclear power are to the modern world. Slavery was how things got done. Life was almost literally unthinkable
   without it.

How does this final item of "cargo" reveal the depth of Babylon's
wickedness?

10. What prophetic act does the mighty angel perform to indicate judgment on Babylon's violence (v. 21)?

11. Babylon is a city founded on violence. Not only the blood of the martyrs. Babylon has been at the center of a network of violence that spanned the world, and all who have been slaughtered on earth have, in a sense, been slaughtered at the behest of Babylon. Where do we see the violence of Babylon revealed in our own society?

~ *Crime* ~

12. How might we live in a way that opposes this violence?

PRAY

Rejoice before God and the Lamb over the fall of the great whore who has drained the life from so many people throughout her violent existence. Offer prayers for all those who are still oppressed by her wickedness, especially those caught in the slave trade that continues to treat human beings like mere cargo designed for profit. Pray that the followers of the Lamb may find strength to oppose the violent systems of Babylon until the day she finally comes down.

GOD'S VICTORY

Revelation 19

In Britain and other parts of the world, weddings can be highly expensive. Even in areas of relative poverty, people still spend tens of thousands of pounds to stage something that seems appropriate to the occasion. There is much about this that I find sad. It feeds commercial interests, and gives to the ceremony itself a flavor which is out of keeping with its real meaning.

But at another level I regard it as an affirmation of something profoundly true about what it means to be human. We are, after all, made male and female in God's image, and in Genesis that is the climax of the whole story of creation. For a man and a woman to come together in marriage, whether they know it or not, is to plant a signpost which says: God's creation is wonderful! God's purposes for it are not over! His plan is going ahead, and we are part of it! Theologians down the ages have always seen the promises made at a wedding, promises of faithfulness through thick and thin, as a proper reflection of God's promises to his world, to the human race and to his own people in particular. A wedding, then, is a glorious symbol. Even when people enter upon it with no thought of God, and with an eye only for the dress, the photographs and the wine, it remains powerful.

All of that is in the background of the great reversal which now takes place in the book of Revelation.

OPEN

What is the most memorable wedding celebration you've ever attended?

650

STUDY

1. *Read Revelation 19:1-10.* How does this passage emphasize the intensity of the celebration that takes place?

   permanent relationship last forever

   shouting cheering .

2. Why is there so much celebration in heaven?

   Justice - evil is vanguished.
   everything is set right.

3. The marriage of the Lamb and his bride is to be the focal point of the marriage of heaven and earth themselves. Who is the "bride" of the Lamb (vv. 7-8)?

   Church,
   Believers.

4. Where are we in this picture of joyful celebration and union?

   marriage feast lasts a long time

5. John himself is so excited by all this that he begins to worship the angel who is revealing it all to him. Why is this a big mistake (v. 10)?

We don't see God directly. He's behind everything. Misapplication of credit.

6. How are we sometimes tempted to make the same mistake John made?

What we see are his instruments - his agents - we are inclined to worship them.

7. *Read Revelation 19:11-21.* What is the significance of the names given to the one riding the white horse (vv. 11, 13)?

faithful and true.

8. It would be as much a mistake to suppose (as some, sadly, have done) that this passage predicts, and legitimates in advance, an actual military battle between followers of Jesus and followers of other gods as it would be to suppose that the reality which corresponds to the monster that comes up from the sea is an actual physical creature with the heads, horns and so on described in chapter 12. The victory here is a victory over all pagan power, which means *a victory over violence itself.*

If not an actual military battle, what do the images in verses 14-16 symbolize?

Spiritual →

9. Jesus himself spoke of victory—but it was not the victory one might expect, over the forces of Rome. Indeed, when others wanted to

fight Rome, he hinted strongly if strangely that this was missing the proper target. The true enemy was the dark power that stood behind Rome and all other pagan empires. Jesus spoke about fighting a battle with the real enemy, the satan, the one who had led all humanity, Israel included, into rebellion against the creator God. And Jesus seems to have believed that the ultimate way to fight this true battle was by giving up his life.

How do we participate in the victory that Jesus has won?

10. What is the ultimate fate of the monster and the false prophet (v. 20)?

lake of fire — torment forever

11. Why do they face such a harsh judgment?

They were unrepentant to the end.

12. Many in our own day are still oppressed by monstrous forces, and the local propaganda machines that promote their cause. Equally, many otherwise well-intentioned people are taken in by the lies and deceits which these systems continue to put out. Revelation 19 stands as a promise to the first, and a warning to the second. Once you understand who Jesus was and is, and the significance of the victory which he has won in his death, there can be no doubt about the final outcome. Monstrous regimes may come and go. Lies and deceits will continue to be spread. We must be on our guard. But the King of kings and Lord of lords will be victorious. In the meantime, there must be no compromise.

How can we help each other to be on guard against falling prey to these lies and deceits?

PRAY

There is much rejoicing in this chapter. Lift up your voice with the great multitude and shout "Salvation and glory and power belong to our God! His judgments are true and just!" Glorify God and the Lamb for triumphing not by violence but by loving self-sacrifice. Pray that you and all God's people will remain faithful to him until the day of the Lamb's great marriage supper, so that you may accept his invitation with joy and be united with him forever.

NOTE ON REVELATION 19:7-9

The idea of such a wedding goes back to the ancient Jewish tradition of Israel as Yahweh's bride in Isaiah 54–55. The whole of the Song of Songs, though at one level simply a spectacular poem of love, has been seen by Jewish and Christian commentators alike as an allegory of the love between God and his people (for Christians, Christ and his people). Now this glorious theme comes to a spectacular completion, and is joined with another ancient theme of celebration: God's great feast, the banquet to which he will invite all and sundry (Isaiah 25:6-10). Jesus himself employed the theme of a king's marriage-supper for his son (Matthew 22:1-14; see too Matthew 25:1-13), and hinted at the further related theme, that of the appropriate clothing for the wedding.

NOTE ON REVELATION 19:20

Being thrown alive "into the lake of fire which burns with sulphur" is an echo of various biblical passages, not least the fate of Sodom and Gomorrah in Genesis 19. An allusion to Genesis 19 can also be found in Revelation 20:9-10.

THE THOUSAND-YEAR REIGN
AND THE FINAL JUDGMENT

Revelation 20

Afer I published my book *Surprised by Hope*, I had a number of letters and emails from people telling me their experiences with thinking
it through, leading study groups on it and in some cases preaching in
the new way I was recommending.

The central point of the book is that, over against a common Western
Christian view that what matters is "going to heaven when you die," the
proper Christian expectation (as it has been from the earliest centuries of
the church) is of a two-stage postmortem reality. First, those who belong
to the Messiah go to be "with him," as Paul says in Philippians 1:23. Then,
at last, Jesus will appear, as heaven and earth come together in a great fresh
act of new creation. That will be the moment of bodily resurrection of the
saints, the moment the dead have been waiting for. Resurrection, the abo-
lition of death itself, giving God's people new bodies to live in God's new
world, is the great hope both of ancient Judaism and of classic Christianity.

A lot of my readers took to this like ducks to water, which was of
course gratifying. But not so for others. One pastor reported that he had
preached enthusiastically on this theme the next Easter Day, only to be
confronted after the service by his leading lay people, extremely put out
because this wasn't the Easter message they were used to hearing.

*Attacks against the Church are
repetitive, contentions*

OPEN

How have you been taught to think about heaven and the afterlife?

— forever – ultimate end

STUDY

1. *Read Revelation 20:1-6.* What happens to the dragon (vv. 1-3)?

    Cast into lake of fire
    Hell - forever

2. We must not forget that "the satan" (which literally means "the accuser") was initially a member of the heavenly council. Though he has fallen from his position, he may still, by God's permission, play a role. The satan's job was always to "accuse" where accusation was due to make sure that (as a good director of public prosecutions) all wrongdoing was exposed. In what ways has the accuser abused and distorted this role?

3. In what specific ways does the accuser try to lead us astray?

4. For what period of time will the dragon be bound and the faithful martyrs reign with Christ (vv. 2, 4)?

    — 1,000 years —

5. Why do those who share in the first resurrection become priests of
   God (v. 6)?

6. The clue to the passage is, I believe, in verse 4: "I saw thrones, with
   people sitting on them, who were given authority to judge." Where
   have we seen such thrones before? In heaven (Revelation 4:1-4), and,
   way back behind that, in Daniel 7, where the "thrones" were for "the
   Ancient of Days" and "the one like a son of man." But Daniel 7 itself
   interprets the latter phrase corporately, so that "the saints of the
   most high" receive the kingdom and the authority to judge.

   It looks as though John is referring not to a thousand-year period
   on earth, but to the heavenly reality which obtains during a particular period. Jesus, according to the whole New Testament, is *already*
   reigning (Matthew 28:18; 1 Corinthians 15:25-28; etc.); and what
   John is saying is that the martyrs *are already reigning with him*. This,
   indeed, is more or less what is said, as well, in Ephesians 2:6, where
   the church is "seated in heavenly places" in the Messiah Jesus. Presumably they aren't just sitting there doing nothing. Perhaps, after
   all, John's millennium does correspond to a more widely known
   early Christian view—though in Ephesians there is no sense that
   this only applies to martyrs.

   If we are already reigning with Christ as well, how do we serve as
   priests of God and Christ to those around us?

7. *Read Revelation 20:7-15.* What is the significance of the satan being
   released after the thousand years are ended (v. 7)?

8. The troops go straight for the camp of the saints, but no battle takes place. What happens instead (vv. 9-10)?

9. How does this picture of the ultimate overthrow of the devil (v. 10) give us hope to face troubles today?

Babylon was overthrown three chapters ago; the two monsters met their doom in chapter 19; now at last the dragon has been overthrown as well, and for good (v. 10). There remain the last great powers: Death and Hades. *Death* is here both the fact and the power of death; *Hades* is the abode of the dead, the place from which they cannot escape except by a great new act of God. In ancient cosmology, the sea was not thought to be part of Hades, so those who died by drowning in the sea, and were never recovered for burial, formed a separate category of the dead. But they too will now be brought to stand before the great white throne, which seems to have replaced the original throne of chapters 4 and 5. Heaven and earth are being shaken, and the throne room itself seems to be under reconstruction.

10. What is the significance of the books that are opened as the dead gather around the throne (vv. 12-15)?

Countless anxious Protestant teachers, worried that this passage somehow does away with justification by faith, miss the point entirely. When Paul speaks of justification by faith, he is talking about

the present reality according to which all those who believe in Jesus
as the risen Lord are already assured of the divine verdict that they
are "in the right," and are also assured thereby that this same verdict
will be issued on the Last Day.

John has mentioned the book of life several times before (3:5;
13:8; 17:8), where it is said to be the Lamb's book of life, and to have
been written before the foundation of the world. This is a vivid way
of safeguarding the truth taught by Jesus in John's Gospel, "You did
not choose me, but I chose you," as well as by Paul in Romans 8:28-
30 and elsewhere. But this, like justification by faith, is subject to
the proviso that the God who chooses is the triune God who works
as Father, Son and Spirit, not as a blind watchmaker or a celestial
bureaucrat. God, the Creator, at last takes his seat for the final judgment. Here, as throughout Scripture, this judgment will be in accor-
dance with the totality of the life that each person has lived. That, it
seems, is what is written in the "books."

11. How does knowing we are in the Lamb's book of life change who we
    are and what we do today?

12. The way in which the verdict of the Last Day corresponds to the
    verdict issued in the present, on the basis of faith alone, is by the
    work of the Spirit. The Spirit produces, in the individual Christian,
    that overall tenor of life (Paul does not suppose that Christians are
    incapable of sinning) which is seeking for glory, honor and immor-
    tality (Romans 2:7).

    How have you seen the Spirit of God working within you to redeem
    and enhance your own thoughts, desires and actions?

PRAY

Celebrate that the greatest enemies of God and his people will one day meet their ultimate defeat. For now, while the devil still seeks to accuse and deceive us, pray that all God's people might find the wisdom and strength to withstand his last flailing attempts to win a battle he has already lost.

NOTE ON REVELATION 20:2-7

What is the "thousand years"? Just as Revelation 16:16 is the only place in Scripture to mention a final great battle at Armageddon, so Revelation 20 is the only passage in Scripture where a millennium is even mentioned. It would be inappropriate for our whole interpretation of the last days to place more emphasis on isolated verses than they do in Scripture itself. In addition, since John has used all kinds of symbolic numbers throughout his book, we should take this number symbolically also. It would be odd if he were suddenly to throw in an obvious round number but expect us to take it literally.

Perhaps above all, and throughout our study of this book, it doesn't do to be too dogmatic about details. We must hold on to the central things which John has made crystal clear: the victory of the Lamb, and the call to share his victory through faith and patience. God will then do what God will then do. Whether we describe the final events as Revelation 20 has done, or as Paul does in Romans 8:18-26 or 1 Corinthians 15:20-28, it is clear that the one who wins the victory is the creator God, who does so to defeat and abolish death itself and so to open the way to the glories of the renewed creation. That is what matters.

NOTE ON REVELATION 20:3

Why is the binding of the satan temporary? There is a pattern here we have noticed, twice already—a kind of interruption to the expected sequence. First, in the sequence of seals, we had to pause between the sixth and the seventh seals; judgment was suspended while the suffering and martyred people of God were sealed (chapter 7). Then, between the sixth and seventh trumpets, we again had to pause, this time while John was given the scroll from which he prophesied about God's witnessing people (chapters 10 and 11). This unexpected pause in chapter 20 also concerns the suffering and martyred people of God, who are again celebrated as the true witnesses, the priest-kings who share the Messiah's rule (v. 6). The satan must be allowed a final moment to accuse, so that in his overthrow it will be clear beyond the slightest doubt that "there is therefore now no condemnation for those in the Messiah Jesus."

NOTE ON REVELATION 20:11

Why does John say that "earth and heaven fled away from his presence"? In 20:12-14 we see Death is destroyed. This means that the processes of bodily corruption and decay are reversed, producing a new "physical" body with "immortal" properties. John told us from early on that God is celebrated as the Creator of the whole world, and indeed that all creation joins in his praise. If creation is not gloriously reaffirmed at the last, God has been finally defeated: the satan has won. But the "new heaven and new earth" in chapter 21 are that glorious reaffirmation.

Earth had been corrupted by the evil done within it, and heaven too had been the place from which the satan had conducted his initial rebellion. Now, with all obstacles to the ultimate goal having been removed, the corrupted versions of earth and heaven can make way for the final reality to which they were advance signposts. The rule of death is at an end; the rule of life is about to begin.

NEW HEAVEN, NEW EARTH, NEW JERUSALEM

Revelation 21:1-21

There are some moments in life when we say to ourselves, "Everything is going to be different now. This is entirely new. This is a whole new world opening up."

We might think of some major life events: birth, marriage, full recovery from a long and dangerous illness, the experience of someone new coming to live with you. John has, on a cosmic scale, such moments in mind as he builds up this breathtaking picture of the new heaven and new earth. "I will be his God and he shall be my son": a final new birth. The holy city is like "a bride dressed up for her husband": a wedding. There will be "no more death or mourning or weeping or pain anymore": the great recovery. And, central to this whole picture, and indeed explaining what it all means, is the great promise: "God has come to dwell with humans." The new, permanent guest.

As with all symbolism, these are signposts pointing into the unknown future; and at every point John is saying, "It's like this, but much, much more so."

OPEN

When has there been a moment in your life when you have said to yourself, "Everything is going to be different now"?

conversion, moving, parenting —
parent of a teenager, grandparent.
loss of parents.

STUDY

1. *Read Revelation 21:1-5.* What does John see coming down out of heaven (v. 2)?

   Holy city, new Jerusalem

2. What does it mean that God will "dwell" with his people (v. 3)?

   accessible, with us. no doubts,
   See him clearly, know fully.
   Complete understanding.

3. Which of the promises offered in verses 3-4 offers you the most comfort and hope right now, and why?

   protection, security, no fear,
   Fear is everpresent — lots to fear
   — emotional pain — fear of being alone

What we have in Revelation 21 and 22 is the *utter transformation* of heaven and earth by means of God abolishing, from within both heaven and earth, everything that has to do both with the as-yet incomplete plan for creation and, more particularly, with the horrible, disgusting and tragic effects of human sin.

4. Up to now, "the one who sits on the throne" has been mentioned only obliquely. He has been there; he has been worshiped; but all the talking has been done by Jesus, or by an angel, or by "a voice from

God is going to take care of us.

heaven." Now, at last, for the first time since the opening statement in 1:8, God himself, directly and without intermediary, addresses John, and through him addresses his churches and ours.

What is the message that comes from the One who sits on the throne himself (v. 5)?

5. What is included in "all things"?

everything is new.

6. What difference should it make in how we live now to know that God's ultimate purpose is to renew all things of this present existence?

Relief — afflictions are temporary pains, uncedventures. Good reminder. Provide purpose

7. *Read Revelation 21:6-21.* How is the New Jerusalem specifically designed to reflect the identity of God's people (vv. 12-14)?

Diverse — God's people — All tribes, all nations.

8. As verse 16 makes clear, the city is not only vast in terms of its footprint—fifteen hundred miles each way. It is also fifteen hundred miles *high.* John, of course, has no thought of what kind of buildings would occupy this extraordinary structure; he is constructing a symbolic universe, not an architect's design. The city will be an enormous, perfect *cube* . . . because that is the shape of the holy

of holies at the heart of the ancient temple in Jerusalem, the place
where God's presence is most palpably found (1 Kings 6:20).

What is the significance of this connection between the holy of holies and the New Jerusalem?

9.   How are the walls of the city decorated (vv. 18-21)?

*Shades of color
— diversity — God' appreciation
of diversity*

10. Why does John go into so much detail describing these walls?

11. This great new reality, the place of God's dwelling on earth, can
never be something that humans make (that takes us back to Babylon, to Babel!), but remains always and forever the gift of God's love
and grace.

How might we live in a way that is open to receiving great gifts from
God rather than always trying to build everything ourselves?

*Have God fight our battles for us
Relying on him — surrender —
Show up, dont think.*

12. The picture we are gazing at in these chapters is certainly a vision of
the ultimate future. Yet, as we have seen from the letters at the start
of the book, there are signs that this reality keeps peeping through
even in the present world of death and tears, of cowards and liars.

I don't have to fix things —

Just as nothing we do in the present is *merely* relevant to the present, but can carry implications into God's future, so nothing in the vision of the future is *merely* future.

How do you see the glory of this future reality peeping through in our world today?

There are positives - there is some progress against hunger, medical breakthroughs.

PRAY

Imagine you are with John, gazing on the beauty of the New Jerusalem, basking in the glory of God's presence. Here there are no more tears, no more sorrow, no more pain, no more death. Simply sit for a few moments before God, then offer him your deepest gratitude for this promise of the complete renewal of all creation. Pray that you might always hold this hope before you, and that you would be attentive to the places where this new reality is already breaking into this present world.

NOTE ON REVELATION 21:1

Why is there "no more sea"? Throughout this book, as in much of the Bible, the sea is the dark force of chaos which threatens God's plans and God's people. It is the element from which the first monster emerged (13:1). It is contained in the first heaven: "contained" both in the sense that it is there as part of the furniture and in the sense that its boundary is strictly limited. But in the new creation there will be no more sea, no more chaos, no place from which monsters might again emerge.

Thank you for the promise of renewal.

GOD AND THE LAMB ARE THERE

Revelation 21:22–22:21

As we reach the end of this most remarkable of books, we realize we have only skimmed it in the interests of time and space. Yet we are aware of the depths we have glimpsed as we have sped by. The sequence of events—the letters, the seals, the trumpets and the bowls, and all that went with and around them—may have merged into one in our memory. It may seem like a glorious, wild, ancient sound, pointing us back to the very dawn of time and the most ancient of Scriptures, and yet also pointing us to things yet to come in God's ultimate future. But, out of this rich confusion of vision and image, two or three notes now stand out, emerging variously from all that has gone before, part of the music and yet with something else to say. Pay attention. Keep these words. I am coming soon. I am coming soon.

OPEN

What have you sensed God trying to say to you in the midst of this remarkable book?

Have hope for a greater justice.

STUDY

1. *Read Revelation 21:22–22:7.* Why are the temple, the sun and the moon absent from the New Jerusalem (21:22-23)?

    No need — God is there.

2. In what way did the ancient temple in Jerusalem serve as a signpost to something greater?

    — There is something greater
    — Worth worshipping

    In what way do the sun and the moon themselves act as signposts in that way?

    A creation, a creator

3. Slowly we rub our eyes, and discover that even the glorious world of Genesis 1 was the beginning of something, rather than an end in itself. It was itself a great signpost, pointing to the world that God always intended to make out of it.

    How does this help us understand and appreciate more deeply the world we live in?

    Not an end itself — point to
    something greater, more perfect.

4. For most of Revelation, "the nations" and their kings have been hostile. They have shared in the idolatry and economic violence of Babylon; they have oppressed and opposed God, his purposes and

    Not the End of the story,

his people. But the earlier hints of God's wider redeeming purpose
now come fully into play.

How will the nations participate in the life of the New Jerusalem
(21:24-26)?

5. Why are the gates of the city never shut (21:25)?

*No fear, calm, demise of evil,
security, no locks on the doors.*

6. That which ruins the beauty and holiness of God's new city is ruled
out by definition. What is specifically mentioned here (21:27)?

*Impurity, Shame, deceit, only
the names of the Saved.*

7. How might we begin to prepare ourselves even now for life in this
holy city?

Repentance – acceptance –

8. Once God's glory has returned to the newly built temple in Ezekiel
43, we discover that this temple is actually a kind of new Eden, from
which a river will flow out to irrigate the world around. Ezekiel saw
in his vision fruit trees on either bank of the river (47:12), with their
fruit for food and their leaves for healing. John, in one of the most
moving reworkings of biblical imagery in his entire book, sees the
river of the water of life flowing, sparkling on its way through the
city streets and out into the countryside beyond. The tree which

grows in profusion on either bank of the river is "the tree of life," the tree which was forbidden to Adam and Eve as they were expelled from the garden. And the "tree of life" is not merely there to provide healing for this person, or that, for this Adam or this Eve.

According to John, what is the purpose of the leaves on the tree (22:2)?

9. From the start of the book we were told that the Lamb's followers were to be a royal priesthood, and now we see what this means. It is from the city, the city which is the bride, the bride which is the Lamb's followers, that healing, restorative stewardship is to flow. This is how the creator God will show, once and for all, that his creation was good, and that he himself is full of mercy.

How might we begin to participate in this healing, redeeming work today?

10. *Read Revelation 22:8-21.* Who beckons Jesus to come (22:17)?

Spirit

bride (church)

11. It is the Spirit that enables the bride to be the bride. It is the Spirit that enables the martyrs to keep up their courage and bear true witness. It is the Spirit who inspires the great shouts and songs of praise. The Spirit goes out from God's throne and, breathing into and then through the hearts, minds and lives of people of every na-

tion, tribe and tongue, returns in praise to the Father and the Lamb. The bride is caught up in that inner-divine life, so that when she says "Come!" to her beloved we can't tell whether this is the Spirit speaking or the bride, because the answer is both.

How is this Spirit empowering you in your life as a follower of Jesus today?

12. How might we live in joyful expectation of the day when Jesus comes?

PRAY

The Spirit awakens in the cloister and the church, in the war zone and the throne room, in the island of exile and the house of torment, in the hearts of men and women, in the dreams of little children, even on the bishops' bench and in the scholar's study, the prayer, the cry, the song, the hope, the love: "Amen! Come, Lord Jesus." Let us join that chorus today and for the rest of our lives until he indeed comes again.

GUIDELINES FOR LEADERS

My grace is sufficient for you.
(2 Corinthians 12:9)

If leading a small group is something new for you, don't worry. These sessions are designed to flow naturally and be led easily. You may even find that the studies seem to lead themselves!

This study guide is flexible. You can use it with a variety of groups—students, professionals, coworkers, friends, neighborhood or church groups. Each study takes forty-five to sixty minutes in a group setting.

You don't need to be an expert on the Bible or a trained teacher to lead a small group. These guides are designed to facilitate a group's discussion, not a leader's presentation. Guiding group members to discover together what the Bible has to say and to listen together for God's guidance will help them remember much more than a lecture would.

There are some important facts to know about group dynamics and encouraging discussion. The suggestions listed below should equip you to effectively and enjoyably fulfill your role as leader.

PREPARING FOR THE STUDY

1. Ask God to help you understand and apply the passage in your own life. Unless this happens, you will not be prepared to lead others. Pray too for the various members of the group. Ask God to open your hearts to the message of his Word and motivate you to action.

2. Read the introduction to the entire guide to get an overview of the topics that will be explored.

3. As you begin each study, read and reread the assigned Bible passage to familiarize yourself with it. This study guide is based on the For Everyone series on the New Testament (published by SPCK and Westminster John Knox). It will help you and the group if you have on hand a copy of the companion volume from the For Everyone series both for the translation of the passage found there and for further insight into the passage.

4. Carefully work through each question in the study. Spend time in meditation and reflection as you consider how to respond.

5. Write your thoughts and responses in the space provided in the study guide. This will help you to express your understanding of the passage clearly.

6. It may help to have a Bible dictionary handy. Use it to look up any unfamiliar words, names or places. The glossary at the end of each New Testament for Everyone commentary may likewise be helpful for keeping discussion moving.

7. Reflect seriously on how you need to apply the Scripture to your life. Remember that the group members will follow your lead in responding to the studies. They will not go any deeper than you do.

LEADING THE STUDY

1. At the beginning of your first time together, explain that these studies are meant to be discussions, not lectures. Encourage the members of the group to participate. However, do not put pressure on those who may be hesitant to speak—especially during the first few sessions.

2. Be sure that everyone in your group has a study guide. Encourage the group to prepare beforehand for each discussion by reading the introduction to the guide and by working through the questions in each study.

3. Begin each study on time. Open with prayer, asking God to help the group to understand and apply the passage.

4. Have a group member read aloud the introduction at the beginning of the discussion.
5. Discuss the "Open" question before the Bible passage is read. The "Open" question introduces the theme of the study and helps group members to begin to open up, and can reveal where our thoughts and feelings need to be transformed by Scripture. Reading the passage first will tend to color the honest reactions people would otherwise give—because they are, of course, supposed to think the way the Bible does. Encourage as many members as possible to respond to the "Open" question, and be ready to get the discussion going with your own response.
6. Have a group member read aloud the passage to be studied as indicated in the guide.
7. The study questions are designed to be read aloud just as they are written. You may, however, prefer to express them in your own words.

   There may be times when it is appropriate to deviate from the study guide. For example, a question may have already been answered. If so, move on to the next question. Or someone may raise an important question not covered in the guide. Take time to discuss it, but try to keep the group from going off on tangents.
8. Avoid answering your own questions. An eager group quickly becomes passive and silent if members think the leader will do most of the talking. If necessary repeat or rephrase the question until it is clearly understood, or refer to the commentary woven into the guide to clarify the context or meaning.
9. Don't be afraid of silence in response to the discussion questions. People may need time to think about the question before formulating their answers.
10. Don't be content with just one answer. Ask, "What do the rest of you think?" or "Anything else?" until several people have given answers to the question.
11. Try to be affirming whenever possible. Affirm participation. Never reject an answer; if it is clearly off-base, ask, "Which verse led you to that conclusion?" or again, "What do the rest of you think?"

12. Don't expect every answer to be addressed to you, even though this will probably happen at first. As group members become more at ease, they will begin to truly interact with each other. This is one sign of healthy discussion.

13. Don't be afraid of controversy. It can be very stimulating. If you don't resolve an issue completely, don't be frustrated. Explain that the group will move on and God may enlighten all of you in later sessions.

14. Periodically summarize what the group has said about the passage. This helps to draw together the various ideas mentioned and gives continuity to the study. But don't preach.

15. Conclude your time together with the prayer suggestion at the end of the study, adapting it to your group's particular needs as appropriate. Ask for God's help in following through on the applications you've identified.

16. End on time.

Many more suggestions and helps for studying a passage or guiding discussion can be found in *How to Lead a LifeGuide Bible Study* and *The Big Book on Small Groups* (both from InterVarsity Press/USA).